DATE DUE

MAY 6 1987			
RETURNED P3 Nov 3 6 1987			
NOV 19 1987			
RETURNED DEC 1 7 2001			
DEC 1 2 2001			

DEMCO NO. 38-298

Natural hazards 2
Catastrophes naturelles
Catástrofes naturales
Стихийные бедствия
Natur-Katastrophen

Avalanche atlas
Illustrated international avalanche classification

Atlas des avalanches
Classification internationale illustrée des avalanches

Atlas de las avalanchas
Clasificación internacional ilustrada de las avalanchas

Атлас лавин
Иллюстрированная международная классификация лавин

Lawinen-Atlas
Bebilderte Internationale Lawinenklassifikation

International Commission on Snow and Ice
of the International Association of Hydrological Sciences

Commission internationale pour la neige et la glace
de l'Association internationale des sciences hydrologiques

Comisión Internacional de la Nieve y el Hielo
de la Asociación Internacional de Ciencias Hidrológicas

Международная Комиссия по Снегу и Лбду Международнуй
Ассоциации Гидрологических Наук

Internationale Kommission für Schnee und Eis
der Internationalen Assoziation für Hydrologische Wissenschaften

Published in 1981 by the United Nations
Educational, Scientific and Cultural Organization
7 place de Fontenoy, 75700 Paris
Printed by Courvoisier S.A., La Chaux-de-Fonds

Publié en 1981 par l'Organisation des Nations Unies
pour l'éducation, la science et la culture,
7, place de Fontenoy, 75700 Paris
Imprimé par Courvoisier S.A., La Chaux-de-Fonds

Publicado en 1981 por la Organización de las Naciones Unidas
para la Educación, la Ciencia y la Cultura
7 place de Fontenoy, 75700 Paris
Impreso por Courvoisier S.A., La Chaux-de-Fonds

Опубликовано в 1981 г. Организацией Объединенных Наций
по вопросам образования, науки и культуры
7, place de Fontenoy, 75700 Париж
Отпечатано в Courvoisier S.A., La Chaux-de-Fonds

Herausgegeben 1981 von der Organisation für Erziehung,
Wissenschaft und Kultur,
7 Place de Fontenoy, 75700 Paris
Gedruckt von Courvoisier S.A., La Chaux-de-Fonds

ISBN 92-3-001696-9
© Unesco 1981
Printed in Switzerland

Preface

In the course of the past fifteen years, Unesco has become increasingly concerned with the study of natural hazards and of the means of protection against them. This has involved not only the promotion of scientific research into the causes and mechanisms of the natural phenomena that cause disasters, and of technological research leading to improved methods of protection, but also the study of the attendant social and economic problems. The basic study of snow and ice mechanics is also part of Unesco's long-term International Hydrological Programme.

Snow avalanches are not the most destructive of natural phenomena—floods and earthquakes take a far heavier toll of life and property each year—but the losses they inflict are nevertheless increasing steadily, with the rapid development of human activities, especially of sport and leisure, in mountainous areas.

Effective action to reduce the losses caused by avalanches, be it through more effective warning, through the more accurate identification of avalanche-risk zones or through protective engineering, must necessarily be based on sound knowledge of the natural phenomenon. The present publication is aimed at this. By presenting a systematic scheme of classification, illustrated by numerous photographs, this *Atlas* will, it is hoped, be of immediate value to all those who, because of their responsibilities or from personal interest, observe and record avalanches.

The classification scheme set forth in this *Atlas* has been drawn up by an international working group of experts, set up by the International Commission on Snow and Ice (ICSI). It is based on experience acquired in many parts of the world and thus provides a framework for the observation and recording of avalanches in a standard form, which will make it easier in the future to compare and collate information and data from different countries. It also constitutes a practical guide for avalanche observers, professional or amateur, which, it is hoped, will give them a clearer insight into these spectacular and dangerous phenomena.

Unesco wishes to express its gratitude to all those who have contributed to the present work. Particular thanks are due to Professor Marcel R. de Quervain, chairman of the Working Group on Avalanche Classification of ICSI, who acted as co-ordinator and general editor, and also to the copyright owners who have authorized Unesco to reproduce their photographs in this publication without charge.

The designations employed and the presentation of material throughout the publication do not imply the expression of any opinion whatsoever on the part of Unesco concerning the legal statuts of any country, territory, city or area or of its authorities, or concerning the delimitation of its frontiers or boundaries.

Préface

Depuis quinze ans, l'Unesco s'intéresse de plus en plus à l'étude des risques naturels et des moyens de s'en protéger. Ces activités consistent non seulement à encourager une recherche scientifique visant à déceler les causes et les mécanismes des phénomènes naturels qui sont à l'origine des catastrophes ainsi qu'une recherche technologique débouchant sur l'amélioration des méthodes de protection, mais également à étudier les problèmes sociaux et économiques connexes. L'étude fondamentale de la mécanique des neiges et des glaces entre également dans le cadre du Programme hydrologique international à long terme de l'Unesco.

Les avalanches de neige ne sont pas les phénomènes naturels les plus destructeurs — les inondations et les tremblements de terre se soldent chaque année par un bilan beaucoup plus lourd en vies humaines et en destructions matérielles — mais les pertes qu'elles entraînent ne cessent néanmoins d'augmenter, parallèlement au rapide développement des activités humaines, en particulier des sports et loisirs, dans les régions montagneuses.

Pour être efficace, toute action visant à réduire les pertes provoquées par les avalanches, qu'il s'agisse de moyens de prévention plus sûrs, de la localisation plus précise des zones exposées aux risques d'avalanches ou de travaux de génie civil, doit nécessairement reposer sur une solide connaissance de ce phénomène naturel. C'est ce but qu'entend servir la présente publication. En offrant un schéma systématique de classification, illustré de nombreuses photographies, le présent Atlas sera, il faut l'espérer, d'une utilité directe pour toutes les personnes qui, en raison des responsabilités qui leur incombent ou de leurs préoccupations personnelles, observent et enregistrent les avalanches.

Le schéma de classification proposé dans le présent Atlas a été mis au point par un groupe international d'experts, créé par la Commission internationale pour la neige et la glace (ICSI). Il est fondé sur l'expérience acquise dans de nombreuses régions du monde et fournit ainsi un cadre de référence pour l'observation et l'enregistrement normalisés des avalanches, ce qui facilitera à l'avenir la comparaison et le rassemblement des informations et données provenant de différents pays. Il constitue également un guide pratique pour les personnes que leur profession ou leur curiosité personnelle conduit à observer de tels phénomènes et vise à leur donner une connaissance plus précise de ces phénomènes spectaculaires et dangereux.

L'Unesco tient à exprimer sa gratitude à toutes les personnes qui ont participé à l'élaboration du présent ouvrage et remercie particulièrement M. de Quervain, président du groupe de travail sur la classification des avalanches de l'ICSI, qui s'est chargé de la coordination des travaux de la mise au point rédactionnelle, de même que les titulaires de droits d'auteur qui ont autorisé l'Unesco à reproduire gratuitement leurs photographies dans la présente publication.

Prefacio

En el curso de los últimos quince años, la Unesco se ha venido interesando cada vez más por el estudio de los riesgos naturales y de los medios de protección contra los mismos. Ello ha implicado no sólo la promoción de investigaciones científicas sobre las causas y los mecanismos de los fenómenos naturales que ocasionan los desastres, y de las investigaciones tecnológicas que permiten mejorar los métodos de protección, sino también el estudio de los problemas sociales y económicos conexos. El estudio básico de la mecánica de la nieve y el hielo forma asimismo parte del Programa Hidrológico Internacional a largo plazo de la Unesco.

Las avalanchas de nieve no son los fenómenos naturales más destructores; inundaciones y terremotos hacen pagar un tributo más pesado de vidas y de bienes cada año, pero las pérdidas que aquéllos infligen aumentan sin embargo progresivamente con el rápido desarrollo de las actividades humanas en las zonas montañosas, especialmente de deportes y distracciones.

Una acción efectiva para reducir las pérdidas ocasionadas por las avalanchas, ya sea por medio de medios de prevención más eficaces, ya sea por medio de una determinación más exacta de las zonas con riesgos de avalanchas o por medio de una ingeniería protectora, debe necesariamente basarse en un conocimiento sólido de este fenómeno natural. Éste es el objetivo de la presente publicación. Cabe esperar que este Atlas, que presenta un esquema sistemático de clasificación, ilustrado con numerosas fotografías, será de valor inmediato para todos aquellos que, por sus responsabilidades o su interés personal, observan y registran las avalanchas.

El esquema de clasificación expuesto en este Atlas ha sido establecido por un grupo internacional de expertos, instituido por la Comisión Internacional de la Nieve y el Hielo (ICSI). Se basa en la experiencia adquirida en muchas partes del mundo y ofrece, por lo tanto, un marco de referencia para la observación y registro de avalanchas en una forma normalizada, lo que facilitará en el futuro la comparación y el cotejo de informaciones y datos de los diferentes países. También constituye una guía práctica para observadores de avalanchas, tanto profesionales como aficionados, a los que, es de esperar, dará una visión más clara de esos espectaculares y peligrosos fenómenos.

La Unesco expresa su gratitud a todos cuantos han contribuido al presente trabajo. En particular da las gracias al Sr. M. R. de Quervain, presidente del grupo de trabajo sobre la clasificación de avalanchas de la ICSI, que actuó como coordinador y revisor general, así como a los propietarios de los derechos de autor que han autorizado a la Unesco a reproducir sus fotografías en esta publicación sin costo alguno.

Предисловие

В течение последних 15 лет ЮНЕСКО проявляет все больший интерес к изучению стихийных бедствий и средств защиты от них. Это привело не только к развитию научных исследований причин и механизмов природных явлений, которые вызывают стихийные бедствия, и техническим исследованиям, ведущим к улучшению методов защиты, но также к изучение сопутствующих соцальных и экономических проблем. Фундаментальные исследования по механике снега и льда также являются частью долгосрочной Международной гидрологической программы ЮНЕСКО.

Снежные лавины – это не самые разрушительные природные явления – гораздо большие потери человеческих жизней и имущества влекут ежегодно наводнения и землетрясения, – но наносимый ими ущерб тем не менее постоянно растет при быстром развитии деятельности человека, особенно спорта и досуга в горных областях.

Эффективные действия для уменьшении ущерба, наносимого лавинами, посредством использования более эффективных систем предупреждения, путем более точного определения лавиноопасных зон или строительства инженерных защитных сооружений, должны обязательно основываться на прочных знаниях об этом природном явлении. Цель настоящей публикации и состоит в этом. Атлас, в котором представлена систематизированная схема классификации, иллюстрированная многочисленными фотографиями, как мы надеемся, принесет непосредственную пользу всем тем, кто в силу своих обязанностей или из личного интереса наблюдает и регистрирует случаи лавин.

Схема классификации, приведенная в Атласе, была составлена Международной рабочей группой экспертов, созданной Международной комиссией по снегу и льду (МКСЛ). Она основывается на опыте, приобретенном во многих частях мира, и обеспечивает, таким образом, рамки для наблюдения и регистрации лавин в стандартной форме, которая упростит в будущем сравнение и сопоставление информации и данных из различых стран. Она также представляет собой практическое руководство для профессионалов или любителей, наблюдающих за лавинами, которое, как мы надеемся, даст им более ясное представление об этих захватывающих и опасных явлениях.

ЮНЕСКО хотела бы выразить свою благодарность всем, кто внес вклад в настоящую работу. Особую благодарность следует выразить г-ну М. де Кервену, председателю рабочей группы по классификации лавин МКСЛ, который координировал работу и осуществлял общую редакцию, а также лицам, позволившим ЮНЕСКО бесплатно перепечатать в этой публикации их фотографии, на которые они имеют авторское право.

Подразумевается, что указания и оформление материала не выражают ни в коей мере мнения ЮНЕСКО относительно юридического положения той или иной страны или территории, их властей или границ этих стран или территорий.

Vorwort

Die Unesco hat sich in den letzten 15 Jahren zunehmend mit der Frage von Natur-
katastrophen und möglichen Schutzmassnahmen befasst. Dies hat nicht nur eine
verstärkte wissenschaftliche Erforschung der Ursachen und Auswirkungen von
Naturkatastrophen und eine schnellere technische Entwicklung besserer Schutzmassnahmen zur Folge, sondern führt auch zu Untersuchungen entsprechender sozialer
und wirtschaftlicher Probleme. Beobachtungen des mechanischen Verhaltens von
Schnee und Eis sind ebenfalls Bestandteil des langfristigen, internationalen
Hydrologie-Programmes der Unesco.

Schneelawinen richten weitaus geringeren Schaden an und verursachen weniger
Opfer an Leben und Eigentum pro Jahr als Überschwemmungen und Erdbeben,
haben aber trotzdem, in Anbetracht der zunehmenden Popularität des Wintersportes,
grössere Verluste zur Folge.

Eine gründliche Kenntnis der Naturgeschehnisse ist notwendig, um wirksamere
Massnahmen zur Verhinderung von Lawinenschäden zu treffen, sowohl durch ein
besseres Warnsystem und eine genauere Kennzeichnung der Gefahrenzonen als auch
Lawinenverbauungen. Dies Werk dient diesem Ziel. Wir hoffen, dass der systematisch
aufgebaute, reich illustrierte Atlas all jenen von grossem Nutzen sein wird, welche
dank ihres Berufes oder auch aus reinem persönlichem Interesse Lawinenbeobach-
tungen anstellen.

Die im Atlas enthaltene systematische Zusammenstellung wurde von einer
internationalen Expertengruppe, welche von der Internationalen Kommission für
Schnee und Eis (ICSI) ernannt wurde, ausgearbeitet. Die hierin gesammelten globalen
Erfahrungen dienen als Grundlage für Beobachtungen und Aufzeichnungen von
Lawinen und werden in Zukunft dazu beitragen, entsprechende Informationen und
Daten aus verschiedenen Ländern zu vergleichen und zusammenzufassen. Der Atlas
dient gleichzeitig als praktischer Führer für den professionellen Lawinenbeobachter
oder auch den Amateur; wir hoffen, dass er ein klareres Bild der so spektakulären und
gefährlichen Naturerscheinung vermittelt.

Die Unesco dankt all jenen welche zu diesem Werke beigetragen haben. Spezieller
Dank gebührt Herrn Dr. M. R. de Quervain, Koordinator und Herausgeber sowie

Vorsitzender der ICSI Arbeitsgruppe für Lawinenklassifizierung, und den Besitzern des Verlagsrechtes, welche die Unesco ermächtigt haben, ihre Fotographien unentgeltlich in dieser Veröffentlichung zu verwenden.

Contents

Frontispiece: Engraving by D. Herrliberger after D. Dürringer, *Topographie der Eydgenossenschaft*, 1754.

Table des matières

Frontispice: Gravure par D. Herrliberger d'après D. Dürringer, *Topographie der Eydgenossenschaft*, 1754.

Indice

Frontispicio: Grabado por D. Herrliberger, tomado de D. Dürringer, *Topographie der Eydgenossenschaft*, 1754.

Содержание

Титульный лист: гравюра Д. Херрлибергера по мотивам работы
Д. Дюррингера, *Topographie der Eydgenossenschaft* 1754.

Inhaltsverzeichnis

Frontispiz: Stich   von   D.   Herrliberger   nach   D.   Dürringer,   *Topographie   der   Eydgenossenschaft*, 1754.

Introduction

In the denomination of avalanches the first terms were coined by the early settlers, who distinguished primarily between dry and wet avalanches. Nowadays the manifold encounters of modern man with this natural phenomenon have brought out the need for a more detailed description of the visible features of avalanches and of their genetic factors. In response to this need, a morphological and genetic avalanche classification, based on proposals that have been made and tested in Switzerland (since 1955), has been developed by a working group[1] of the International Commission on Snow and Ice (of the International Association of Hydrological Sciences). This classification was published (*Bulletin of the International Association of Hydrological Sciences*, Vol. XVIII, No. 4, 1973) and has been tentatively adopted as the International Avalanche Classification.

The present publication has been prepared to illustrate the various characteristics of avalanches, and to relate them to the international classification. In the first part, this classification is presented and explained. The second part comprises a collection of photographs from several countries, among them some of the most impressive avalanche pictures available, which, together with the analytical legends, constitute a field guide for observers. The snow classification has been included to assist observers to give a complete description of the snow and avalanche conditions.

International Commission on Snow and Ice

---

[1] Working Group on Avalanche Classification: M. R. de Quervain, Chairman (Switzerland); L. de Crécy (France); E. R. LaChapelle (United States of America); K. Lossev (Union of Soviet Socialist Republics); M. Shoda (deceased 1974, replaced by T. Nakamura) (Japan).

Introduction

Dans la terminologie des avalanches, les premiers termes ont été forgés par les populations qui se sont installées à l'origine dans ces régions et qui distinguaient principalement entre les avalanches sèches et les avalanches humides. A l'heure actuelle, l'homme moderne s'est trouvé tant de fois aux prises avec ce phénomène naturel qu'il est apparu nécessaire de concevoir une description plus détaillée des caractéristiques apparentes des avalanches ainsi que de leurs facteurs génétiques. A cette fin, un groupe de travail[1] de la Commission internationale pour la neige et la glace (de l'Association internationale des sciences hydrologiques) a mis au point une classification morphologique et génétique des avalanches, fondée sur des propositions qui avaient été formulées et mises à l'essai en Suisse (depuis 1955). Cette classification a été publiée (*Bulletin de l'Association internationale des sciences hydrologiques*, XVIII, 4/1973) et a été adoptée à titre provisoire en tant que Classification internationale des avalanches.

La présente publication a été élaborée en vue d'illustrer les diverses caractéristiques des avalanches en se reportant à la classification internationale. La première partie est consacrée à la présentation et à l'explication de cette classification. La deuxième partie contient une collection de photographies provenant de plusieurs pays, parmi lesquelles figurent quelques-unes des images les plus impressionnantes qui puissent exister, avec les légendes qui accompagnent ces photos, elle constitue un guide pratique pour les observateurs. La classification des neiges y a été insérée afin de permettre aux observateurs de donner une description complète des conditions dans lesquelles se produit l'avalanche et de l'état de la neige.

Commission internationale pour la neige et la glace

---

[1] Groupe de travail sur la classification des avalanches: M. R. de Quervain, président (Suisse); L. de Crécy (France); E. R. LaChapelle (Etats-Unis d'Amérique); K. Lossev (U.R.S.S.); M. Shoda (décédé en 1974 et remplacé par T. Nakamura) (Japon).

Introducción

En la denominación de las avalanchas, la visión de los antiguos pobladores ha formado los primeros términos, distinguiendo principalmente las avalanchas secas y las avalanchas húmedas. El encuentro múltiple de la vida moderna con este fenómeno natural hace necesaria una descripción más detallada de las características visibles de las avalanchas y de sus factores genéticos.

Para responder a esta necesidad, un grupo de trabajo[1] de la Comisión Internacional de la Nieve y el Hielo (que forma parte de la Asociación Internacional de Ciencias Hidrológicas) ha desarrollado un sistema de clasificación de las avalanchas basado en propuestas formuladas y puestas a prueba en Suiza (desde 1955). Esta clasificación fue publicada (*Boletín de la Asociación Internacional de Ciencias Hidrológicas*, vol. XVIII, n.° 4, 1973) y ahora ha sido adoptada provisionalmente como Clasificación Internacional de Avalanchas.

Esta publicación ha sido preparada para presentar fotográficamente las características de las avalanchas y para ordenarlas según la clasificación internacional. En la primera parte se presenta y se explica la clasificación. La segunda parte contiene una colección de fotografías de diversos países, entre las cuales figuran algunas de las fotografías más impresionantes que existen de este fenómeno, que forman, con las leyendas, una guía para el observador. También se ha incluido la clasificación de la nieve, para facilitar al observador la descripción completa de las condiciones en que se producen las avalanchas y del estado de la nieve.

Comisión Internacional de la Nieve y el Hielo

---

[1] Grupo de trabajo sobre la clasificación de avalanchas: M. R. de Quervain, presidente (Suiza); L. de Crécy (Francia); E. R. LaChapelle (Estados Unidos de América); K. Lossev (URSS); M. Shoda (fallecido en 1974, sustituido por T. Nakamura) (Japón).

Введение

В описаниях лавин первые термины создавались ранними поселенцами, которые, в первую очередь, делали различие между сухими и мокрыми лавинами. Сегодня многочисленные столкновения современного человека с этим природным явлением сделали необходимым более подробное описание видимых черт лавин и их генетических факторов. В целях удовлетворения этой потребности рабочая группа[1] Международной комиссии по снегу и льду (Международная ассоциация гидрологических наук) разработала морфологическую и генетическую классификацию лавин, основанную на предложениях, которые были выдвинуты и опробованы в Швейцарии (с 1955 г.). Эта классификация была опубликована (Bulletin of the International Association of Hydrological Sciences, XVIII, 4/1973 г.) и была в предварительном порядке утверждена в качестве Международной классификации лавин.

Настоящая публикация была подготовлена для того, чтобы проиллюстрировать различные характерные черты лавин и соотнести их с Международной классификацией. Эта классификация приводится с пояснениями в первой части. Вторая часть содержит коллекцию фотографий из нескольких стран, причем в их число входят несколько наиболее представительных из имеющихся снимков лавин, которые вместе с аналитической легендой составляют практическое руководство для наблюдателей. Классификация снега была включена для того, чтобы помочь наблюдателям дать полное описание снежных и лавинных условий.

Международная комиссия по снегу и льду

---

[1] Рабочая группа по классификации лавин Международной комиссии по снегу и льду. М. Р. де Кервен, Председатель (Швейцария). Л. де Креси (Франция). Э. Р. Ла Шапель (США). К. Лосев (СССР). М. Шода (скончался в 1974 г., замещен Т. Накамурай) (Япония).

Einführung

In der Bezeichnungsweise der Lawinen haben die Eindrücke der frühen Siedler die ersten Begriffe geformt, wobei zunächst trockene und nasse Lawinen unterschieden wurden. Die vielfältige Begegnung des heutigen Lebens mit dieser Naturgewalt ruft nach einer differenzierteren Beschreibung der sichtbaren Erscheinungen der Lawinen und der sie verursachenden Bedingungen.

Um diesem Bedürfnis zu entsprechen, ist durch eine Arbeitsgruppe[1] der Internationalen Kommission für Schnee und Eis (zugehörig der Internationalen Assoziation für Hydrologische Wissenschaften) eine *Lawinenklassifikation* geschaffen worden, die an in der Schweiz vorgebrachte und erprobte Vorschläge (seit ca 1955) anschliesst. Diese Klassifikation wurde publiziert (Bulletin der Internat. Assoziation für Hydrologische Wissenschaften XVIII, 4/1973) und ist versuchsweise eingeführt als Internationale Lawinenklassifikation.

Die vorliegende Ausgabe wurde zusammengestellt, um die verschiedenen Charakteristiken der Lawinen im photographischen Bild zu zeigen und sie der internationalen Klassifikation zuzuordnen. Im ersten Teil ist diese Klassifikation dargelegt und erläutert. Der zweite Teil enthält eine Sammlung von Photographien aus verschiedenen Ländern, — darunter einige der eindrücklichsten Lawinenaufnahmen — die zusammen mit den Bilderläuterungen einen Leitfaden für Beobachter bilden. Die Schneeklassifikation ist beigefügt worden, um dem Beobachter die vollständige Beschreibung der Schnee- und Lawinenverhältnisse zu erleichtern.

Internationale Kommission für Schnee und Eis

---

[1] Arbeitsgruppe für Lawinenklassifikation: M. R. de Quervain, Vorsitzender (Schweiz); L. de Crécy (Frankreich); E. R. LaChapelle (U.S.A.); K. Lossev (U.S.S.R.); M. Shoda, verstorben 1974, Nachfolger T. Nakamura (Japan).

Classification and recording of avalanches and snow data   I

Classification et enregistrement des données sur les avalanches et la neige

Clasificación y registro de datos sobre avalanchas y nieve

Классификация и регистрация данных о лавинах и снеге

Klassifikation und Aufzeichnung von Lawinen- und Schneedaten

The International Avalanche Classification

1   Principles of the avalanche classification

1.1   Scientific purpose: to observe and record avalanche characteristics in a condensed form suitable for the study of the statistical and physical laws governing avalanche phenomena.

1.2   Practical purpose: the classification enables the user to describe an observed or expected avalanche in simple terms, easily understood by other persons familiar with the system. Avalanche warning, rescue operations and engineering works are aided by the common language provided by the classification.

1.3   The code for the morphological classification (Section 2.3) is an abbreviated notation that is particularly useful for the recording and transmission of observations.

1.4   General classification scheme: the features of an avalanche and its genetic conditions are subdivided as follows:

	Descriptive (qualitative) characteristics
	Types of avalanches
Immediate phenomenon of avalanche	*Morphological classification*
	Measurable (quantitative) characteristics
	Avalanche effects (damage, victims)
	Terrain conditions
	Stratification of snow cover
Genetic conditions of avalanche formation	Weather (recent/actual)
	Triggering mechanism
	Genetic classification (classification of avalanche conditions)

There are close interrelations between the immediate avalanche features and the genetic conditions. Terrain conditions, for example, are included in both. In the present treatment, measurable characteristics and avalanche effects are not dealt with in detail. Emphasis is given to the morphological classification. As regards the genetic classification, a tentative scheme is given for the most significant and well-established relations.

2 Morphological classification of avalanches

2.1 *Classification scheme*

Zone	Criterion	Alternative characteristics, denominations and code	
Zone of origin	A Manner of starting	A1 starting from a point (loose-snow avalanche)	A2 starting from a line (slab avalanche) A3 soft A4 hard
	B Position of sliding surface	B1 within snow cover (surface-layer avalanche)	B4 on the ground (full-depth avalanche)
		B2 (new-snow B3 (old-snow fracture) fracture)	
	C Liquid water in snow	C1 absent (dry-snow avalanche)	C2 present (wet-snow avalanche)
Zone of transition (free and retarded flow)	D Form of path	D1 path on open slope (unconfined avalanche)	D2 path in gulley or channel (channelled avalanche)
	E Form of movement	E1 snow dust cloud (powder avalanche)	E2 flowing along the ground (flow avalanche)
Zone of deposition	F Surface roughness of deposit	F1 coarse (coarse deposit) F2 angular F3 rounded blocks clods	F4 fine (fine deposit)
	G Liquid water in snow debris at time of deposition	G1 absent (dry avalanche deposit)	G2 present (wet avalanche deposit)
	H Contamination of deposit	H1 no apparent contamination (clean avalanche)	H2 contamination present (contaminated avalanche) H3 rock debris, H4 branches, soil trees H5 debris of structures

2.2 *Comments on the morphological classification*

2.2.1 **Definition of zones**

Zone of origin

Zone in which the appearance of an avalanche is characterized by the manner of starting. For a slab avalanche it comprises the distance down to the pressure fracture; for
a loose-snow avalanche there is no sharp lower limit. A distance of 100 m will include
the zone of origin in most cases.

Zone of transition

Flow is independent of manner of starting. The velocity may be increasing, steady or
decreasing. No particular avalanche deposit is visible after the avalanche has passed,
except for snow retained by roughness of terrain (for example, in narrow gullies).

Zone of deposition

A natural deposit is produced by loss of energy due to friction. The zone of deposition
may exhibit a wide range of slope angles, including a reverse slope. The position of its
boundary with the transition zone may vary considerably from one avalanche to
another in the same path according to the snow quality (dry, wet, dense, etc.). For
powder avalanches the zone of deposition is the sediment zone of the snow cloud.

2.2.2 **Criteria and alternative characteristics**

General

For each criterion two alternative characteristics are offered, of which some are subdivided into sub-characteristics. If the subdivision is not used (when discrimination is
not possible or not needed) the upper common term is applied. In some cases the
alternative characteristics are mutually exclusive; in others they may be observed
simultaneously. It often happens that not all the characteristics are determined, or
that not all of them are of interest for a given problem. This flexible system allows the
observer to use only the relevant terms in oral or written communications, in which
the terms to be used are those in brackets. (See illustrations). The capital letters
attributed to the criteria, combined with figures for the characteristics, can be used as
a code for the recording and transmission of data (see Section 2.3).

Detailed comments:
A. Manner of starting

Loose snow avalanche. The starting point may be determined by a falling object
(stone, ice chunk, etc.) or by a skier. In the latter case the point fracture mechanism
is obscured.

Slab avalanche. 'Starting from a line' does not exclude the possibility of the movement being propagated as an invisible fracture from a single point of initiation. The
term 'slab' is often used synonymously with 'slab-avalanche', but this should be
avoided unless there is no doubt about the correct meaning. Distinction between soft

and hard slab: in a *soft slab* the broken snow layer is very soft or soft (see Snow Classi-fication). The slab disintegrates into loose material immediately after the start. In a *hard slab* the broken snow layer is medium hard, hard or very hard. Chunks or angular blocks of snow are carried longer distances, depending on the roughness of the avalanche paths. Slab fracture may be observed without a subsequent avalanche (it is often related to the slow gliding movement of wet snow—see Figures 63 and 64). When well lubricated by melt-water, a snow glide may turn into an avalanche move-ment. This process is denoted by the term 'glide avalanche' (see Figure 18).

B. Position of sliding surface

Within snow cover. 'New snow' in 'new-snow fracture' means a uniform layer of snow more or less continuously deposited during the five days preceding the avalanche and not implying granular snow types. A new-snow fracture is present even if the surface conditions of the immediately underlying old snow have favoured the fracture (e.g. surface hoar, loose surface, icy crust). The sliding surface of an 'old-snow fracture' lies *within* the old snow (snow older than about five days), thus contributing old snow to the avalanche at the fracture line. Whether the majority of avalanching snow consists of new snow and whether the new-snow load actually caused the fracture are not relevant in this respect.

On the ground. Even when a snow veil or some snow patches are left on the ground after passage of the avalanche, owing to roughness of the ground surface, 'full-depth avalanche' should nevertheless be noted.

C. Liquid water in snow at fracture

A 'wet-snow avalanche' implies the presence of liquid water throughout the avalanching layer, otherwise the avalanche is 'dry' or 'mixed'. Discrimination may be difficult unless the weather conditions (temperature, radiation, rain) are taken into account. The classic term 'ground avalanche', formerly used either for 'wet-snow avalanche' or for 'full-depth avalanche', is now reserved for heavy, wet, spring avalanches that entrain masses of rock or soil.

D. Form of path

Many channelled avalanches start as unconfined avalanches and are concentrated into one or several channels only in the lower part of their courses. If the dominant part is channelled (the fracture area is often funnel-shaped) they are characterized as 'channelled'; otherwise a mixed type is reported for the whole path.

The *longitudinal profile* of an avalanche path is often very significant (change in slope angle, intermediate steps, cascade formation, etc.). A quantitative description of the profile is generally better and more feasible than an elaborate classification of all possible terrain profiles.

E. Form of movement

No distinction is made between a translatory gliding movement ($v > \sim 1 \ m/s$) and a flowing, crumbling or rolling movement. In the starting zone the movement always follows the ground (flow avalanche).

Mixed types are very frequently observed. 'Mixed flow and powder avalanche', 'flow avalanche with powder component', 'powder avalanche with flow component' are possible ways to characterize mixed types. A movement detached from the ground—either of powdery or flowing type—may be called a 'cascade'.

Snow creep and glide with slow velocities and negligible dynamic effects ($v < 1\ cm/s$) are not classified as avalanche movements (see Figures 62–66).

F. Surface roughness of deposit

A deposit is considered to be *coarse* if the mean dimension of the clods is larger than about *30 cm,* otherwise it is *fine.*

Angular blocks are pieces of the original snow deposit, and thus usually characterize a hard slab fracture. *Rounded clods* also include irregular chunks.

G. Liquid water in snow debris

Large avalanches that are dry in the zone of origin may pick up wet snow in the lower parts of their tracks and thus change their character. Wet snow in debris leads to hard and solid deposit, almost impermeable to air, an important factor in rescue work and avalanche clearing.

H. Contamination of deposits

Deposits with separate clean and contaminated zones are frequent and are classified as 'mixed'. Besides an evident contamination, avalanches may contain faintly visible or invisible admixtures of foreign material (dust, organic particles, radioactive substances, etc.). These are not taken into account in the classification. Some deposits contain a large proportion of debris (rock, soil). If such deposits are the result of landslides or floods they are not classified as avalanche deposits even if they contain snow.

2.3   *Code for the morphological classification*

2.3.1   General

Symbol for criterion: capital letter. Symbol for characteristic: figure. General use of figures: unknown, not needed or not applicable, 0; specific pure characteristics, 1–6; mixed characteristics, 7 or 8; reference to special remarks outside the code system, 9. Example *in tabulated form:*

A	B	C	D	E	F	G	H	J	Remarks:
3	9	0	7	0	0	0	4	0	B9: 3 fracture levels.

In cursory form, referring to certain criteria only: D7, A3, H4, B9 (B9: 3 fracture levels). Each group consists of a letter followed by a figure; the order of the groups is not important.

2.3.2   Code for morphological classification

Criterion	Symbols		
Characteristics	Criterion	Characteristics	
		pure	mixed
Manner of starting	A		
Loose snow avalanche		1	
Slab avalanche (general)		2	7
Slab avalanche soft		3	
Slab avalanche hard		4	
Position of sliding surface	B		
Surface-layer avalanche (general)		1	
Surface-layer avalanche, new snow fracture		2	
Surface-layer avalanche, old snow fracture		3	8 } 7
Full-depth avalanche		4	
Liquid water in snow at fracture	C		
Absent: dry-snow avalanche		1	7
Present: wet-snow avalanche		2	
Form of path	D		
Unconfined avalanche		1	7
Channelled avalanche		2	
Form of movement	E		
Powder avalanche (dominant)		1	7
Flow avalanche (dominant)		2	
Surface roughness of deposit	F		
Coarse deposit (general)		1	
Coarse deposit angular blocks		2	7
Coarse deposit rounded clods		3	
Fine deposit		4	
Liquid water in deposit	G		
Absent: dry deposit		1	7
Present: wet deposit		2	
Contamination of deposit	H		
Clean deposit		1	7
Contaminated deposit (general)		2	
Contaminated by rock, debris, soil		3	
Contaminated by branches, trees		4	8
Contaminated by debris of structures		5	
Triggering mechanism[1]	J		
Natural release		1	
Human release (general)		2	
Human release, accidental		3	
Human release, intentional		4	

[1] This criterion is an element of the genetic classification. Since the triggering mechanism within the given alternatives is known in most cases and is important for many problems, it is added to the morphological code.

3   Genetic classification of avalanches
(Classification of avalanche conditions)

3.1   *General*

In the strict sense of the term, a genetic classification should classify each avalanche according to its origin. However, since most avalanches are the result of various inter-acting genetic factors that differ in nature (e.g. snowfall, wind, temperature), a classi-fication based on one dominant factor per class would be appropriate in a restricted number of cases only, such as avalanches related only (or principally) to new snowfall, to wind, to high temperature or to poor stratification. A different approach—i.e., proceeding from the genetic factor to the resulting avalanche effect—has therefore been adopted in compiling a catalogue of avalanche conditions and of their effects.

A record of the pertinent conditions of an observed avalanche permits a genetic analysis and explanation of the event; more important, the study of these conditions makes it possible to evaluate the avalanche danger prior to actual events and, in certain cases, to make a *quantitative* (deterministic or statistical) *avalanche forecast.*

3.2   *Classification of avalanche conditions*

Condition	Effect on avalanche activity
A. Fixed framework	
(1) *Terrain conditions*	
(1.1) *Relative altitude*	
General topographic situation:	Effect depending on latitude and level of surrounding mountains.
—zone of crest and high plateaux	Strong wind influence, cornices, local slab avalanches.
—zone above timberline and belows crests	Extended areas of slab avalanche formation.
—zone below timberline	Reduced wind influence. Reduced slab avalanches, soft type prevailing.
(1.2) *Slope (ψ)*	
>35°	Formation of loose-snow avalanches possible.
>25°	Formation of slab avalanches possible.
>15°	Stationary or accelerated flow.
<20°	Retarded flow or deposition. (Slush avalanches can occur at very low angles.)
(1.3) *Orientation of slope*	
—relative to sun	On shady slopes enhanced dry slab-avalanche formation. On sunny slopes enhanced wet-avalanche formation.
—relative to wind	On lee slopes increased drift accumulation; enhanced slab-ava-lanche formation. The reverse on windward slopes.
(1.4) *Configuration of terrain*	
—open, even slopes	Unconfined avalanches.
—channels funnels, ridges	Channelled, concentrated, confined avalanches.
—changes in gradient	Slab or loose-snow fracture on convex gradients.
—steps	Powder avalanches, cascade formation.

Condition	Effect on avalanche activity
(1.5) *Roughness*	
—smooth ground	Snow glide (on wet ground); full-depth avalanches favoured.
—protruding obstacles (rocks, cross ridges)	Surface layer avalanches above level of roughness.
—vegetation	Grass: promotes snow glide, and full-depth avalanches. Shrubs: reduces avalanche formation if not snow covered. Forests: prevent avalanche formation if dense.

B. Genetic variables

Condition	Effect on avalanche activity
(2) *Recent weather* (period~5 days back)	
(2.1) *Snowfall*	Increasing load. Increasing mass of low stability. *Most important factor in avalanche formation.*
—type of new snow	Fluffy snow: loose-snow avalanches. Cohesive snow: slab avalanches.
—depth of daily increments of new snow	Increasing instability with snow depth ($\psi > \sim 25°$). New or old snow fracture.
—intensity of snowfall	Progressive instability with higher intensity, promoting new snow fracture and increasing risk on gentle slopes.
(2.2) *Rain*	Promotion of wet loose-snow avalanches or soft slab avalanches. Mixed snow and land slides.
(2.3) *Wind*	Two effects: enhanced local snow deposit (see 1.3) and increased brittleness of snow.
—direction	Increased slab-avalanche formation on leeward slopes. Formation of cornices.
—velocity and duration	Local slab-avalanche formation increased with increasing velocity and duration.
—(2.4) *Thermal conditions* Significant factors: Temperature and free water content of snow.	Ambivalent effect on strength and stress, i. e. on avalanche formation: Rise of snow temperature causes crisis, but ultimately stability. Rise of free water content promotes avalanche formation.
—air temperature	Similar effect on all exposures.
—solar radiation	Dominant effect on sun-exposed slopes.
—thermal radiation	Cooling of snow surface at night and in shadow; important with cloudless sky. Promotion of surface and depth-hoar formation (see 3.2).
(3) *Old snow conditions* Integrated past weather influences of the whole winter season	
(3.1) *Total snow depth*	Not a dominant factor in avalanche danger. Influences mass of full-depth avalanches. Important in compaction and metamorphism of snow cover. Surface-layer avalanches, see (1.5).
(3.2) *Stratification* Sequence of strength	Stability governed by weakest layer with respect to state of stress.
—surface layer	Looseness (surface hoar), brittleness, roughness important to subsequent snowfall.
—interior of snow cover	Old-snow fractures caused by *weak intermediate layers* (old surfaces) and *depth hoar*.

Condition	Effect on avalanche activity

(4) *Triggering mechanism*

(4.1) *Natural release*
—internal influences   Natural avalanche.
—external (non-human) influences   Spontaneous avalanche.
                                                                   Naturally triggered avalanche.

(4.2) *Human release*

—accidental triggering   —Accidental avalanche (triggering).
—intentional release   —Artificial avalanche (triggering).

3.3   *Comments on genetic conditions and effects*

(1.1) Relative altitude

The altitude effect is very complex. It involves variation with altitude of: temperature, radiation, wind, precipitation, length of winter, vegetation, general topography. The effect is relative in so far as it is variable with respect to latitude and climatic region.

(1.2) Slope

Owing to the variable strength and friction of snow, there is a great variation in slope angle related to the starting and flowing conditions of avalanches. The given figures represent common values of inclination but not the extremes. Large and hazardous slab avalanches often originate in the range between 35° and 40° slope. There is an overlap between steady or accelerate flow and retarded flow and deposition.

(1.5) Roughness of ground

Snow glide may provoke large fissures in the snow cover without resulting in avalanches. In avalanche-protection techniques, a particular classification of roughness is used, characterized by a 'glide-factor' N.

(2) Recent weather

Avalanches caused by recent weather conditions and running in new snow have been called 'direct-action avalanches' (type B2). Avalanches involving a long-term development (metamorphism) in the old snow cover (see old snow conditions, stratification (3.2)) have been called 'climax avalanches' (type B3 or B4).

(2.1) Depth of new snow

Most catastrophic avalanches affecting settled zones and a high percentage of winter-sports avalanches are related to *new snow deposition*. New snow depth is the most important factor in avalanche warning. A clear distinction should be made between the sum of daily snowfall measurements (daily new-snow increments), the settled depth of a new-snow layer built up during several days and the increase of total snow depth (three different figures).

(2.3) Wind

Brittleness of drift deposit causes local peak stresses and brittle fractures. As a rule, cornices themselves are not the most dangerous spots for slab fracture. They indicate the prevailing wind conditions, but fracture usually occurs below cornices. From certain regions an upper limit of wind influence is reported. Higher areas may be deprived of snow by extremely high winds to such an extent that avalanche activity is reduced there.

(2.4, 3.2) Thermal conditions and stratification

Temperature variations of the snow, whether caused by the transfer of sensible or latent heat or by incoming and outgoing radiation, have an immediate and irreversible effect on the mechanical properties of snow. Besides this, they influence the densification of snow and the mode and intensity of snow metamorphism, i. e. the transformation of snow crystals from feathery new snow to rounded or faceted old-snow grains. With a strong temperature gradient, *depth hoar* (at the very surface, also surface hoar) is formed, representing a coarse granular and brittle structure of comparatively low cohesion. In the absence of a temperature gradient, snow is transformed into a cohesive material of smaller rounded grains. These irreversible secondary temperature effects have a delayed action on avalanche conditions. Together with snowfall and wind, they control the stratification of the snow cover and are responsible for the formation of weak and strong layers. A rise of the snow temperature to the melting point causes profound and irreversible changes of the mechanical properties of snow, primarily a pronounced reduction in strength.

4   Complete avalanche survey

The detailed investigation of an avalanche requires, in addition to the morphological classification, a minimum set of measured quantitative data. This is important for analysing avalanche accidents, preparing avalanche maps and planning avalanche protection. A full survey of an avalanche event covers the morphological character-istics as well as the genetic conditions.

Checklist for a complete avalanche survey

1 Notes on the field survey

Names of observers, date, weather.

2 Maps, sketches, photographs

The general outlines of the avalanche(s) are marked on maps (scale 1:5,000 to 1:50,000). Sketches are useful for the recording of dimensions and other characteristics (scale 1:500 to 1:5,000). Photographs are of documentary value. Air photographs are of great value (particularly if they include the starting zone). As the quality of photographs can only be checked afterwards, sketches should always be made.

3 Notes on avalanche data[1]

Location: region, community, mountain slope.
Altitude: zone of origin and of deposition.
Date and time of event.
Morphological classification.
Dimensions of avalanche: Width and length of fractured area. Average (and local) thickness or depth of fractured layer. Length and width of zone of transition. Dimensions (including depth) of avalanche deposit (volume). Dimensions of zone of air blast.
Orientation and angle of slope: zone of origin, zone of transition, zone of deposit (total longitudinal profile).
Dynamic characteristics: velocity, pressure effects (see paragraph 5 below).

4 Notes on genetic conditions

Terrain conditions: roughness of terrain, vegetation, geological conditions.
Recent weather (~five days back): precipitation, wind, temperature.
Old snow conditions: stratification (snow profile).
Triggering mechanism: natural, human.

5 Damage

Casualities: number and names of persons involved (including eyewitnesses). Persons killed, missing, injured, rescued unharmed. Circumstances of accident.
Structural damage: type, number of objects, degree of destruction.
Interruption of traffic: roads, railways, transmission lines.
Damage to forests, pastures, loss of animals.
Behaviour of protective structures.

6 Rescue operations

Action of witnesses. Participating organizations. Number of helpers. Logistics, progress and success of operations. Location of victims (means, depth, time). Condition, medical treatment of victims.

---

[1] If not covered by maps and sketches.

Snow classification (abstract)

Under the title 'The International Classification for Snow' a full classification of snow, adopted by the International Commission on Snow and Ice (1952), was published as *Technical Memorandum No. 31* by the Associate Committee on Soil and Snow Mechanics, National Research Council, Ottawa, Canada, 1954.

An abstract of this classification related to deposited snow only is reproduced here in Tables 1, 2 and 3. It enables the user to record in a standardized written or graphic form the snow stratification and the snow surface conditions related to avalanche release. Figure 1 presents a snow profile that uses the system.

The symbols in this classification are not connected with the avalanche code and should be used separately. For certain quantities, various symbols are in use.

TABLE 1. Classification of deposited snow.

Feature	Symbol	Subclassification *					Remarks
		a or 1	b, 2	c, 3	d, 4	e, 5	
Grain shape (see Figures 48 to 53)	F	original shape / new snow	partly branched / snow slightly settled felt-like	rounded / old snow (·)	faceted / old snow	ribbed, cup shaped, depth hoar	Fc: open circle for melt metamorphism (optional); From left to right progressive metamorphism
Grain size mean diameter (mm)	D	<0,5 very fine	0,5-1 fine	1-2 medium	2-4 coarse	>4 very coarse	Numbers to be used for mm only
Free water (%)	W	dry	moist	wet	very wet	slush	Wb: snow sticky; Wc: water visible; Wd: water running off; We: saturated
Cohesion (N/m²)	K	very low	low	medium	high	very high	Ice lenses / layers. Scale for strength and hardness, see below
Hardness	R	very soft	soft	medium hard	hard	very hard	
Density (kg/m³)	G, ϱ						Density values only
Snow temperature (°C)	T						Indicate position of measurement

* Optionally letter, figure or measured value.

Approximative comparative scale for strength (cohesion) and hardness

Observation, measurement	a, very low	b, low	c, medium	d, high	e, very high	
Cohesion K (kN/m²)	0-1	1-7,5	7,5-25	25-50	>50	
Ram hardness (Ramsonde 4 cm Ø) R (N)	0-20	20-150	150-500	500-1000	>1000	10 N ≈ 1 kp
Hand test (object can be pushed in the snow with moderate force (≈ 30 N))	fist	4 fingers	1 finger	pencil	knife	

TABLE 2. Snow surface conditions (see Figures 50 to 61)

Feature	Symbol	a, (1)	b, (2)	c, (3)	d, (4)	e, (5)
Surface deposits	V	surface hoar	soft rime	hard rime	glazed frost	
Surface roughness	S	smooth	wavy	concave furrows	convex furrows	random furrows
Penetrability (cm)	P	<0,5	0,5-2	2-10	10-30	>30

* Depth of vertical penetration (cm)   PS : Skier on one ski
PP : Man on one foot
PR : First section of standard ramsonde

TABLE 3. Symbols for snow cover measurements

Feature (m, cm, mm)	Vertical	Perpendicular to slope		
Co-ordinate from ground	H, h	M, m, D, d		
Total depth	HS, Hs	MS, Ms, DS, Ds		
Daily new snowfall	HN, Hn			
Water equivalent of snow cover (mm)	HW, Hw			

Inclination of slope (degrees, grades)	N, ψ° (g)
Specific snow-covered area (tenth)	Q
Age of deposit (hours, days, years)	A

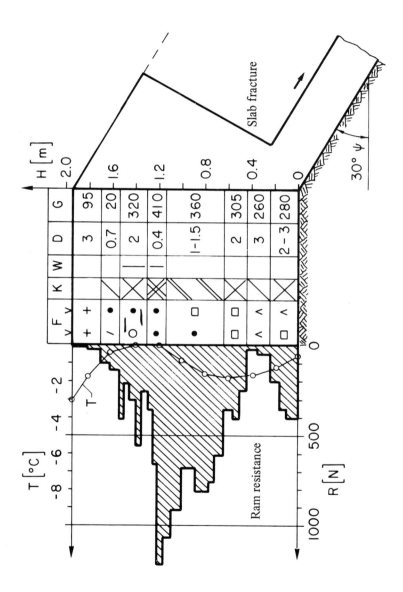

F<small>IG</small>. 1. Representation of a snow profile at an avalanche fracture. For the symbols and figures see pages 41–42. See also Figure 49, snow profile in transmitted light.

La classification internationale des avalanches

1 Principe de la classification des avalanches

1.1 But scientifique: les caractéristiques observées permettant de décrire une avalanche sont présentées sous une forme condensée qui facilite l'étude des statistiques et physiques régissant le phénomène.

1.2 But pratique: la classification met l'usager en mesure de décrire une avalanche observée ou prévue avec des termes simples, facilement compris par toute personne familiarisée avec le système. La prévision des avalanches, les opérations de sauvetage, les actions de génie civil sont facilitées par le langage commun que représente la classification.

1.3 Le code pour la classification morphologique (section 2.3) est une notation abrégée particulièrement utile pour transmettre les observations.

1.4 Schéma général de classification: les éléments se rapportant à une avalanche et à ses conditions génétiques sont subdivisés comme suit:

Faits concernant le phénomène avalanche en lui-même	Caractéristiques descriptives
	Types d'avalanches
	Classification morphologique
	Caractéristiques mesurables (quantitatives)
	Effets de l'avalanche (dommages, victimes)
Conditions génétiques de la formation des avalanches	Conditions du terrain
	Stratification du manteau neigeux
	Conditions météorologiques (récentes et présentes)
	Mécanisme de déclenchement
	Classification génétique (classification des facteurs d'avalanche)

Entre les faits concernant le phénomène avalanche lui-même et les facteurs génétiques, il y a d'étroites relations; les conditions du terrain, par exemple, font partie de ces deux aspects. Dans le présent travail les caractéristiques mesurables et les effets de l'avalanche ne sont pas étudiés en détail. L'accent est mis sur la classification morphologique. Pour ce qui est de la classification génétique, on donne un essai de schéma pour les relations les plus importantes et les mieux établies.

2 Classification morphologique des avalanches

2.1 *Schéma de classification*

Zone	Critères	Caractères distinctifs, dénomination et code	
Zone de départ	A Mode de départ	A1 partant d'un point (avalanche de neige sans cohésion)	A2 partant d'une ligne (avalanche de plaque) A3 plaque tendre A4 plaque dure
	B Position du plan de glissement	B1 à l'intérieur du manteau neigeux (avalanche superficielle) B2 cassure dans la neige fraîche B3 cassure dans la vieille neige	B4 sur le sol (avalanche de fond)
	C Eau liquide dans la neige	C1 absente (avalanche de neige sèche)	C2 présente (avalanche de neige mouillée)
Zone de transition	D Tracé du parcours	D1 parcours sur une pente ouverte (avalanche de versant)	D2 parcours dans un couloir ou une gorge (avalanche de couloir)
	E Type de mouvement	E1 nuage de poussière de neige (avalanche de neige poudreuse)	E2 coulant le long du sol (avalanche coulante)
Zone de dépôt	F Rugosité superficielle du dépôt	F1 grossière (dépôt grossier) F2 blocs F3 boules anguleux arrondies	F4 fine (dépôt fin)
	G Eau liquide dans les détritus de neige au moment du dépôt	G1 absente (dépôt sec)	G2 présente (dépôt humide)
	H Souillure du dépôt	H1 pas d'autres matériaux visibles (avalanche propre)	H2 souillure visible (avalanche souillée) H3 rochers, H4 branches, cailloux, arbres sols H5 débris d'ouvrages

2.2 *Commentaires sur la classification morphologique*

2.2.1 **Définition des zones**

Zone de départ

Zone dans laquelle l'existence d'une avalanche se manifeste par son mode de départ. Pour une avalanche de plaque elle comprend la distance jusqu'à la ligne de rupture à la pression; pour une avalanche de neige sans cohésion il n'y a pas de limite inférieure précise. En général, la zone de départ s'étendra sur moins de 100 mètres dans le sens de la pente.

Zone de transition

Ecoulement indépendant du mode de départ. La vitesse peut être croissante, stable ou décroissante. Il n'y a pas de dépôt particulier après le passage de l'avalanche, hormis la neige retenue par la rugosité du terrain (par exemple dans les couloirs étroits).

Zone de dépôt

Un dépôt naturel se produit en raison de la perte d'énergie due au frottement. La zone de dépôt peut s'étendre sur une large gamme de pentes, y compris des pentes inverses. La position de sa limite avec la zone de transition peut varier considérablement d'une avalanche à une autre dans le même couloir, selon l'état de la neige (sèche, humide, dense, etc.). Pour une avalanche de neige poudreuse, la zone de dépôt est la zone de sédimentation du nuage de neige.

2.2.2 **Critères et caractères distinctifs**

Généralités

Pour chaque critère, deux caractères distinctifs sont proposés, dont certains sont subdivisés en sous-caractères. Si la subdivision n'est pas utilisée (distinction impossible ou inutile), on applique le terme commun de rang supérieur. Dans certains cas les caractères distinctifs s'excluent mutuellement, dans d'autres ils sont observables simultanément. Il arrive souvent qu'on n'a pas déterminé tous les caractères ou qu'ils ne représentent pas tous un intérêt pour un problème donné. Le système souple proposé permet à l'observateur d'utiliser seulement les termes qui conviennent dans les communications écrites ou orales, les termes entre parenthèses étant les seuls à utiliser (voir les illustrations). Les lettres majuscules attribuées aux critères, en combinaison avec des chiffres indiquant le caractère distinctif, peuvent être utilisées comme un code pour l'enregistrement et la transmission de données (voir section 2.3).

Commentaires détaillés
A. Mode de départ

Avalanche de neige sans cohésion. Le point de départ peut provenir de la chute d'un objet (rocher, fragment de glace, etc.) ou d'un skieur. Dans ce dernier cas le mécanisme de la fracture ponctuelle est peu apparent.

Avalanche de plaque. Les mots «partant d'une ligne» n'excluent pas que le mouvement se soit propagé par une ligne de fracture invisible depuis un point isolé. Le terme «plaques» est souvent utilisé comme synonyme «d'avalanche de plaques». Cela doit être évité à moins qu'il n'y ait pas de doute possible sur le véritable sens. Distinction entre plaques tendres et plaques dures: *plaque tendre:* la couche de neige qui a cassé est très tendre ou tendre (voir la classification de la neige). La plaque se désintègre en un matériel sans cohésion immédiatement après le départ de l'avalanche. *Plaque dure:* la couche de neige qui a cassé est mi-dure, dure ou très dure. Des fragments ou des blocs anguleux de cette neige sont transportés sur des distances plus ou moins longues selon la rugosité du parcours de l'avalanche. Des cassures de plaques peuvent être observées sans qu'il s'ensuive une avalanche (phénomène qui est souvent lié à un lent glissement de la neige humide) (voir fig. 63, 64). Lorsque ce mouvement de glissement est bien lubrifié par l'eau de fonte, il peut se transformer en mouvement d'avalanche. Ce processus est décrit par le terme «avalanche de glissement» (voir fig. 18).

B. Position du plan de glissement

A l'intérieur du manteau neigeux. L'appellation «neige fraîche» dans l'expression «cassure dans la neige fraîche» définit un niveau uniforme de neige déposé de manière plus ou moins continue dans les cinq jours qui précèdent la date de l'avalanche et ne comprenant pas de neige de type granulaire. Il y a «cassure dans la neige fraîche» même si les conditions de surface de la vieille neige immédiatement sous-jacente ont favorisé la cassure (par exemple givre de surface, neige à gros grains, croûte glacée). Le plan de glissement d'une «cassure dans la vieille neige» se trouve à l'intérieur de la vieille neige (neige plus ancienne qu'environ 5 jours). Il y a donc participation de la vieille neige à l'avalanche le long de la ligne de fracture. Il importe peu en l'occurrence que la plus grande partie de la neige partie en avalanche soit de la neige fraîche ou que la surcharge due à la neige fraîche soit la cause réelle de la fracture.

Sur le sol. Si, après le passage de l'avalanche, un voile de neige ou quelques traînées de neige sont restées sur le sol en raison de la rugosité de sa surface, l'avalanche n'en doit pas moins être notée «avalanche de fond».

C. Eau liquide dans la neige à la cassure

Le terme «avalanche de neige mouillée» implique que de l'eau liquide est présente dans la couche qui se met en mouvement; sinon l'avalanche serait «sèche» ou «mixte». La distinction peut être difficile si on ne considère pas les conditions météorologiques (température, rayonnement, pluie). Le terme classique d'«avalanche terrière», autrefois utilisé pour «avalanche de neige mouillée» ou pour «avalanche de fond», est maintenant réservé à des avalanches de printemps, en neige lourde et mouillée, qui entraînent des masses de sol ou de rochers.

D. Tracé du parcours

Beaucoup d'avalanches de couloir partent comme des avalanches de versant et sont concentrées dans un ou plusieurs couloirs seulement dans la partie basse de leur trajectoire. Si la plus grande partie du parcours est canalisée (la zone de rupture est souvent en forme d'entonnoir) elles sont notées comme avalanches «de couloir», autrement on relate un type mixte pour l'ensemble du parcours.

Le profil longitudinal du parcours d'une avalanche est souvent très significatif (changement dans l'angle de pente, succession de gradins, formation de cascade). Une description quantitative du profil de l'avalanche est en général meilleure et mieux utilisable qu'une classification élaborée de tous les profils de terrain possibles.

E. Type de mouvement

On n'a pas fait de distinction entre un mouvement de glissement par translation ($v > 1$ m/s) et un mouvement d'écoulement, d'émiettement ou de roulement. Dans la zone de départ, le mouvement suit toujours le sol (avalanche coulante).

Des types mixtes sont très fréquemment observés: «avalanche mixte coulante et poudreuse», «avalanche coulante avec une composante poudreuse», «avalanche poudreuse avec une composante coulante» sont des expressions possibles pour caractériser ces types mixtes. Un mouvement détaché du sol — du type «poudreuse» ou «coulante» — peut être appelé «cascade». Le glissement ou la reptation de la neige avec de faibles vitesses et des effets dynamiques négligeables ($v > 1$ cm/s) ne sont pas classés comme des mouvements d'avalanche (voir fig. 62–66).

F. Rugosité superficielle du dépôt

Un dépôt est considéré comme *grossier* si la dimension moyenne des mottes est supérieure à environ *30 cm*; autrement il est *fin*.

Les *blocs anguleux* sont des morceaux de la couche de neige d'origine, et caractérisent donc une rupture de plaque dure. Les *boules arrondies* comprennent aussi des fragments irréguliers.

G. Eau liquide dans les détritus de neige

Les grandes avalanches qui sont sèches dans la zone de départ peuvent entraîner de la neige mouillée dans la partie basse de leur parcours et changer leur caractère. Lorsque les détritus renferment de la neige mouillée, ils se transforment en dépôts durs et solides, presque imperméables à l'air — facteur d'importance en cas de sauvetage ou de déneigement après l'avalanche.

H. Souillure des dépôts

Il y a souvent des dépôts présentant des zones propres et des zones souillées nettement séparées. On les classe comme «mixtes».

A côté de celles dont la souillure est évidente, certaines avalanches peuvent comporter, de manière invisible ou peu visible, des inclusions de matériaux étrangers (poussière, particules organiques, substances radioactives, etc.). Elles ne sont pas prises en considération dans la classification. Certains dépôts comportent une forte proportion de détritus solides (rochers, sols). Si de tels dépôts sont causés par des glissements de terrain ou des inondations, on ne les classe pas comme dépôts d'avalanche, même s'ils contiennent de la neige.

2.3   *Code pour la classification morphologique*

2.3.1   **Généralités**

Symbole pour les critères: lettre majuscule. Symbole pour les caractères distinctifs: chiffre. Utilisation générale des chiffres: inconnu, inutile, ou non applicable, 0; caractères spécifiques purs, 1 à 6; caractères mixtes, 7 ou 8; référence à des remarques spéciales qui échappent au champ du code, 9. Exemple sous forme de tableau:

A	B	C	D	E	F	G	H	J	Remarques:
3	9	0	7	0	0	0	4	0	B9: 3 niveaux de rupture.

Sous forme succincte, en s'en tenant à quelques caractéristiques seulement: D7, A3, H4, B9 (B9: 3 niveaux de rupture). Chaque indication comporte une lettre et un chiffre; l'ordre des indications est sans importance.

2.3.2   **Codes de classification morphologique**

Critères Caractères distinctifs	Symboles		
	Critères	Caractères distinctifs	
		Purs	Mixtes
Mode de départ	A		
Avalanche de neige sans cohésion		1	7
Avalanche de plaque (en général)		2	
Avalanche de plaque tendre		3	
Avalanche de plaque dure		4	
Position du plan de glissement	B		
Avalanche superficielle (en général)		1	
Avalanche superficielle avec rupture dans la neige fraîche		2	8 / 7
Avalanche superficielle avec rupture dans la vieille neige		3	
Avalanche de fond		4	
Eau liquide dans la neige à la rupture	C		
Absente: avalanche de neige sèche		1	7
Présente: avalanche de neige humide		2	
Tracé du parcours	D		
Avalanche de versant		1	7
Avalanche de couloir		2	
Type de mouvement	E		
Avalanche de neige poudreuse (dominante)		1	7
Avalanche coulante (dominante)		2	
Rugosité superficielle du dépôt	F		
Dépôt grossier (en général)		1	
Dépôt grossier avec blocs anguleux		2	7
Dépôt grossier avec boules arrondies		3	
Dépôt fin		4	
Eau liquide dans le dépôt	G		
Absente: dépôt sec		1	7
Présente: dépôt humide		2	

| Critères | Symboles | | |
| Caractères distinctifs | Critères | Caractères distinctifs | |
		Purs	Mixtes
Souillure du dépôt	H		
Dépôt propre		1	
Dépôt souillé (en général)		2	7
Dépôt souillé par des rochers, des sédiments du sol		3	
Dépôt souillé par des branches, des arbres		4	8
Dépôt souillé par des débris d'ouvrages		5	
Mode de déclenchement[1]	J		
Déclenchement naturel		1	
Déclenchement dû à l'homme (en général)		2	
Déclenchement dû à l'homme (accidentel)		3	
Déclenchement dû à l'homme (volontaire)		4	

[1] Cette caractéristique est un élément de la classification génétique. Comme le mode de déclenchement est connu dans les divers cas donnés la plupart du temps et comme il est important pour de nombreux problèmes, on l'a ajouté au code morphologique.

3   Classification génétique des avalanches
(classification des facteurs d'avalanche)

3.1   *Généralités*

Une classification génétique au sens strict devrait classer les avalanches d'après leur origine. Mais, comme la plupart des avalanches sont le produit de l'interaction entre divers facteurs génétiques, de nature différente (par exemple des chutes de neige, le vent, la température) une classification basée sur un seul facteur dominant par classe ne serait utilisable que pour un nombre restreint d'avalanches (avalanches dues seulement ou principalement à une chute de neige, du vent, à la température ou à une stratification dangereuse). C'est pourquoi on a préféré une autre manière de procéder, qui consiste à établir un catalogue des facteurs d'avalanche et de leurs effets.

En enregistrant les conditions régnantes lors d'une avalanche observée on peut procéder à une analyse génétique et à une explication de l'événement; et — plus important encore — l'étude de ces conditions permet d'évaluer le danger avant que l'événement ne se produise et de conduire à une *prévision* quantitative (déterministe ou statistique) *des avalanches*.

3.2   *Classification des facteurs d'avalanche*

Facteur	Effets

A. Facteurs permanents

(1) *Caractéristiques du terrain*

(1.1) *Altitude relative*

Situation topographique générale	Effet dépendant de la latitude et de l'altitude des montagnes environnantes.
—zones de crêtes et de hauts plateaux	Forte influence du vent, corniches, avalanches de plaques localisées.
—zones au-dessus de la limite de la forêt et sous les crêtes	Grandes zones de formation d'avalanches de plaques.
—zones en dessous de la limite de la forêt	Influence réduite du vent. Moins d'avalanches de plaque, surtout du type de plaque tendre.

(1.2) *Déclivité (ψ)*

>35°	Possibilité de formation d'avalanches de neige sans cohésion.
>25°	Possibilité de formation d'avalanches de plaque.
>15°	Ecoulement d'avalanche stationnaire ou accéléré.
<20°	Ecoulement retardé ou dépôt. (Des avalanches de neige très mouillée peuvent se produire sur des pentes très faibles.)

(1.3) *Orientation du versant*

—relative au soleil	Les pentes à l'ombre favorisent la formation d'avalanches de plaques sèches. Les pentes au soleil favorisent la formation d'avalanches de neige mouillée.
—relative au vent	Sur les pentes sous le vent, accumulation de neige soufflée; favorise la formation d'avalanches de plaque. Côté au vent: l'inverse.

(1.4) *Configuration du terrain*

—pentes ouvertes uniformes	Avalanches de versant.
—couloirs, entonnoirs, arêtes —changement de pentes	Avalanches de couloir, avalanches concentrées, canalisées, cassures de plaques ou de neige sans cohésion dans les zones convexes.
—seuils	Avalanches de neige poudreuse, formation de cascades.

(1.5) *Rugosité*

—sol lisse	Reptation de la neige (sur sol mouillé); favorise les avalanches de fond.
—obstacles en relief (rochers, arêtes transversales)	Avalanches superficielles au-dessus du niveau des obstacles.
—végétation	Herbe: favorise la reptation et les avalanches de fond. Broussailles: réduit la formation d'avalanches si elles ne sont pas recouvertes par la neige. Forêt: empêche la formation d'avalanches si elle est dense.

B. Facteurs variables

(2) *Conditions météorologiques récentes* (pendant les 5 jours précédents)

(2.1) *Chute de neige*

	Accroît la charge. Accroît la masse à faible stabilité. *Le plus important facteur d'avalanche.*
—type de neige fraîche	Neige duveteuse: avalanches de neige sans cohésion. Neige cohérente: avalanches de plaque.

Facteur	Effets
—épaisseur des accroissements	L'instabilité croît avec la profondeur de la neige ($\psi > 25°$). Cassure dans la vieille neige ou dans la neige fraîche.
—intensité des chutes de neige	Instabilité croissante avec l'intensité; favorise les cassures dans la neige fraîche; étend le danger vers les pentes faibles.
(2.2) *Pluie*	Favorise les avalanches de neige mouillée sans cohésion, ou les avalanches de plaque tendre. Glissements mixtes neige et terre.
(2.3) *Vent*	Deux effets: favorise des accumulations locales de neige (voir 1.3) et augmente la fragilité de la neige.
—direction	Accroît la formation d'avalanches de plaque côté sous le vent. Formation de corniches.
—vitesse et durée	Accroissement de la formation locale d'avalanches de plaque si la vitesse et la durée du vent augmentent.
(2.4) *Facteurs thermiques*	
Facteurs significatifs: température et teneur en eau de neige	Double effet sur la résistance mécanique et les efforts subis, c'est-à-dire sur la formation des avalanches. Une élévation de la température de la neige provoque un danger mais, à terme, la stabilité. Une augmentation de la teneur en eau libre facilite la formation d'avalanches.
—température de l'air	Effet similaire à toutes les expositions.
—rayonnement solaire	Effet dominant sur les pentes exposées au soleil.
—rayonnement thermique	Refroidissement de la surface de la neige la nuit et à l'ombre; important par ciel sans nuages. Provoque la formation de givre de surface et de givre de profondeur (voir 3.2).
(3) *Etat de la neige ancienne*	
Influence de l'ensemble des conditions climatiques au cours de toute la saison d'hiver	
(3.1) *Epaisseur totale de la neige*	N'est pas un facteur dominant pour le danger d'avalanche. Influe sur la masse des avalanches de fond. Important pour le tassement et la métamorphose du manteau neigeux. Avalanches superficielles (voir 1.5).
(3.2) *Stratification*	
Ordre de succession des résistances mécaniques	La stabilité dépend de la couche la moins résistante par rapport aux contraintes.
—couche superficielle	Le manque de cohésion (givre de surface), la fragilité, la rugosité sont importants pour les chutes de neige ultérieures.
—intérieur du manteau neigeux	Cassures dans la vieille neige causées par des niveaux intermédiaires peu résistants (anciennes surfaces) et par le givre de profondeur.
(4) *Mécanisme de déclenchement*	
(4.1) *Déclenchement naturel*	Avalanche naturelle.
—influences internes	Avalanche spontanée.
—influences externes (non humaines)	Avalanche déclenchée naturellement.
(4.2) *Déclenchement anthropique*	
—déclenchement accidentel	Avalanche (à déclenchement) accidentel(le).
—déclenchement volontaire	Avalanche (à déclenchement) artificielle.

3.3   *Commentaires sur les facteurs génétiques et leurs effets*

(1.1) L'altitude relative

L'effet de l'altitude est très complexe. Il concerne la température, le rayonnement, le vent, les précipitations, la durée de l'hiver, la végétation, la topographie générale. Cet effet est relatif dans la mesure où il dépend de la latitude et du climat de la région.

(1.2) La déclivité

Le degré de déclivité à partir duquel les avalanches se déclenchent et s'écoulent varie considérablement, étant donné que la résistance mécanique et le frottement de la neige sont eux-mêmes très variables. Les chiffres avancés représentent des valeurs courantes de la pente mais non des extrêmes. De grosses plaques dangereuses se détachent souvent sur des pentes inclinées à 35°–40°. Il y a chevauchement entre les valeurs favorisant l'écoulement continu ou accéléré et celles provoquant le ralentissement et l'arrêt.

(1.5) La rugosité du sol

La reptation de la neige peut provoquer de larges fissures dans le manteau neigeux sans qu'il en résulte des avalanches. En génie paravalanche on utilise une classification particulière de la rugosité caractérisée par un «facteur de glissement» N.

(2) Les conditions météorologiques récentes

Des avalanches qui ont leur source dans les conditions météorologiques récentes et qui se développent dans des couches de neige fraîche, ont été appelées «avalanches d'effet direct» (type B2). Des avalanches qui tiennent à une longue évolution (métamorphisme) au sein du vieux manteau neigeux [voir «Etat de la neige ancienne, stratification (3.2)] ont été appelées «avalanches climactiques» (type B3 ou B4).

(2.1) Epaisseur de neige fraîche

La plupart des avalanches catastrophiques affectant des zones habitées et une grande partie des avalanches intéressant les sports d'hiver se rapportent à des chutes de neige fraîche. L'épaisseur de neige fraîche constitue le facteur le plus important en matière de prévision des avalanches.

Il faut faire une distinction nette entre la somme des mesures journalières de chutes de neige (accroissements quotidiens en neige fraîche), l'épaisseur après tassement de la couche de neige fraîche constituée en plusieurs jours et l'accroissement de l'épaisseur totale de la neige (trois valeurs numériques différentes).

(2.3) Vent

La fragilité des couches de neige déposées par le vent entraîne des fractures sous l'accumulation des tensions locales. Il est de règle que les cassures de plaques ne se produisent pas aux corniches elles-mêmes qui réflètent les conditions atmosphériques et celles du vent en particulier, mais elles interviennent généralement à l'aval des corniches. Dans certaines régions on observe qu'il y a une limite supérieure à l'effet du vent. Des hauts pays peuvent être privés de neige en raison de vents extrêmement forts, au point qu'il s'y produit très peu d'avalanches.

(2.4) et (3.2) Facteurs thermiques et stratification

Les variations de température de la neige, provoquées soit par transfert de chaleur sensible ou latente, soit par rayonnement entrant ou sortant, ont un effet immédiat et irréversible sur les propriétés mécaniques de la neige. De plus, elles déterminent l'augmentation de la densité et l'intensité et les modalités du métamorphisme qui affecte la neige (transformation de cristaux de neige fraîche en vieux grains arrondis ou anguleux). Dans un gradient fort de la température, il se forme du *givre de profondeur* (il y a aussi, à la surface, du *givre de surface*). Ces types de neige ont une structure cassante de gros grains, et leur cohésion est relativement faible. En l'absence de gradient de température, la neige est transformée en un matériau plus ou moins compact, composé de petits grains arrondis. Ces effets secondaires irréversibles de la température agissent à retardement sur la formation des avalanches. Avec les chutes de neige et le vent, ils déterminent la stratification du manteau neigeux et sont à l'origine de la formation des couches faibles et des couches compactes. Un réchauffement de la neige jusqu'au point de fusion amène des changements profonds et irréversibles de ses propriétés mécaniques, en particulier une diminution prononcée de la solidité.

4   Etude complète d'une avalanche

Un examen détaillé d'une avalanche demande, outre la classification morphologique, un minimum de données quantitatives mesurées. Cela est important pour l'analyse des accidents d'avalanche, la préparation des cartes (de zones d'avalanches) et la réalisation de projets pour la protection contre l'avalanche.

Une étude complète d'une avalanche comprend aussi bien les caractéristiques morphologiques que les conditions génétiques.

Liste de référence pour une étude complète d'avalanche

1 Notes sur l'étude in situ

Nom des observateurs, date, le temps qu'il fait.

2 Cartes, dessins, photographies

La situation générale de l'avalanche est indiquée sur des cartes (échelle: 1/5000 à 1/50 000). Des croquis sont particulièrement utiles pour noter les dimensions et les caractéristiques (échelle: 1/500 à 1/5000). Les photographies ont valeur de document. Les photographies aériennes sont d'un grand intérêt (surtout si elles couvrent la zone de départ). Comme la qualité des photographies ne peut se révéler qu'après coup, il faut toujours faire des croquis.

3 Notes sur les données relatives à l'avalanche[1]

Localisation: région, commune, versant de la montagne.
Altitude: des zones de départ et de dépôt.
Date et heure de l'avalanche.
Classification morphologique.
Dimensions de l'avalanche: Largeur et longueur de la zone de fracture, épaisseur ou profondeur moyennes (et locales) de la couche fracturée. Longueur et largeur de la zone de transition. Dimensions (dont profondeur) du dépôt de l'avalanche (volume). Dimensions de la zone de souffle.
Orientation et pente du versant: zone de départ, zone de transition, zone de dépôt (profil longitudinal total).
Caractéristiques dynamiques: vitesse, effets de pression [voir (5)], dégâts.

4 Notes sur les facteurs génétiques

Caractéristiques du terrain: rugosité, végétation, conditions géologiques.
Conditions météorologiques récentes (dans les 5 jours précédents): précipitations, vent, température.
Etat de la vieille neige: stratification (profil de neige).
Mode de déclenchement: naturel, humain.

5 Dégâts

Personnes affectées: nombre et nom des personnes concernées, y compris témoins oculaires, victimes, disparus, personnes blessées ou retrouvées saines et sauves. Circonstances de l'accident.
Dommages causés aux biens: nature et nombre des objets, degré de destruction.
Interruption des communications: routes, chemins de fer, lignes de transmissions électriques ou téléphoniques.
Dommages causés aux forêts et pâturages, pertes de bétail.
Comportement des ouvrages de protection.

6 Opérations de secours

Action des témoins. Organisations ayant participé. Nombre de sauveteurs. Organisation logistique, progrès et succès des opérations. Localisation des victimes (moyens de recherche, profondeur, moment de leur découverte). Etat des victimes et soins qu'elles ont reçus.

---

[1] Autant que ces renseignements ne sont pas déjà donnés par les cartes et croquis.

Classification de la neige (résumé)

En 1954, le Comité associé sur la mécanique des sols et de la neige, organe du Conseil national de la recherche (Ottawa) a publié dans son mémorandum n° 31, sous le titre «Classification internationale pour la neige» une classification complète de la neige, adoptée en 1952 par la Commission internationale pour la neige et la glace.

On a reproduit ici un résumé de cette classification, limitée à la seule neige déposée. Il permettra à l'utilisateur de décrire, sous forme écrite ou graphique standardisée, la stratification de la neige et l'état de la surface de la neige en relation avec le déclenchement des avalanches.

Les symboles utilisés dans cette classification n'ont aucun lien avec le code de classification des avalanches et ils sont à utiliser indépendamment. Pour certains éléments quantitatifs, on fait usage de divers symboles.

TABLEAU 1. Neige déposée

Caractère	Symbole	Classification secondaire*					Remarques
		a ou 1	b, 2	c, 3	d, 4	e, 5	
Forme des grains (voir figures 48-53)	F	forme originale / neige fraîche	partiellement ramifiée / neige un peu tassée, feutrée	grains arrondis / vieille neige	grains anguleux / vieille neige	cannelée gobelets givre de profondeur	Fc : cercle ouvert : métamorphose de fonte (facultatif) / De gauche à droite métamorphose intensifiée
Taille des grains : diamètre moyen (mm)	D	<0,5 très fine	0,5-1 fine	1-2 moyenne	2-4 gros grains	>4 très gros grains	Chiffres à utiliser pour les mm seulement
Eau libre (%)	W	neige sèche	humide	mouillée	très mouillée	détrempée	Wb : neige collante / Wc : eau visible / Wd : eau s'écoule / We : neige saturée
Cohésion (N/m²)	K	très faible très tendre	faible tendre	moyenne	élevée dure	très élevée très dure	Échelle de cohésion et de dureté ; voir ci-dessous
Dureté	R	très faible très tendre	faible tendre	moyenne	élevée dure	très élevée très dure	Lentilles / Couches de glace
Densité (kg/m³)	G, ç						Valeurs numériques seulement
Température de la neige (°C)	T						Indiquer position de mesure

* Au choix lettre, chiffre ou valeur mesurée

Échelle approximative et comparative pour la cohésion et la dureté

Observation, mesure	a, très faible	b, faible	c, moyenne	d, élevée	e, très élevée	
Cohésion K (kN/m²)	0-1	1-7,5	7,5-25	25-50	>50	
Résistance à la sonde de battage 4 cm Ø R (N)	0-20	20-150	150-500	500-1000	>1000	10 N ≈ 1 kp
Test à la main (objet poussé dans la neige avec une force modérée ; environ 30 N)	poing	4 doigts	1 doigt	crayon	lame de couteau	

TABLEAU 2.   Etat de la surface de la neige (voir fig. 50 à 61)

Caractère	Symbole	a, (1)	b, (2)	c, (3)	d, (4)	e, (5)
Dépôt de surface	V	givre de surface, rosée blanche	givre mou	givre dur	verglas	
Rugosité en surface	S	lisse	ondulée	creux concaves	bosses convexes	érodée irrégulièrement
Pénétrabilité en surface (cm)*	P	<0,5	0,5-2	2-10	10-30	> 30

* Profondeur de pénétration verticale (cm):   PS Skieur sur un ski
PP Homme sur un pied
PR Première section de la sonde de battage

TABLEAU 3.   Symboles pour mesures du manteau neigeux

Caractère (m, cm, mm)	Selon la verticale	Selon la perpendiculaire au sol		
Coordonnées à partir du sol	H, h	M, m, D, d	Pente de la surface (degrés, grades)	N, ψ° (g)
Hauteur totale	HS, Hs	MS, Ms, DS, Ds	*Surface en neige* Surface totale (dixièmes)	Q
Chutes de neige quotidiennes	HN, Hn			
Équivalent en eau (mm)	HW, Hw		Âge du dépôt (heures, jours, années)	A

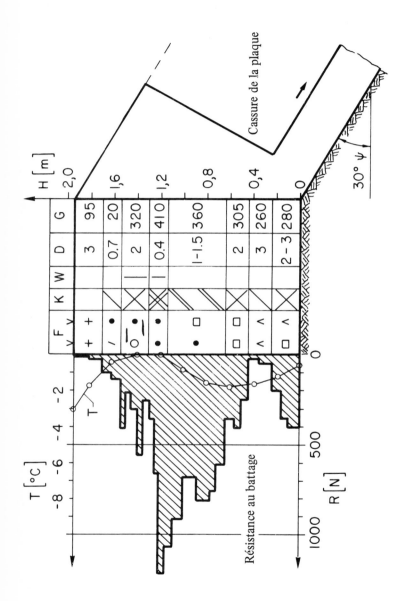

Fig. 1. Représentation d'un profil de neige pris près de la cassure d'une avalanche de plaque. (Symboles et mesures, voir pages 58 et 59. Voir aussi fig. 49, profil de neige dans lumière transmise.)

Clasificación internacional de avalanchas

1 Principios de la clasificación de avalanchas

1.1 Finalidad científica: observar y registrar en forma resumida las características descriptivas que ayudan a determinar las leyes estadísticas y físicas que rigen la actividad de las avalanchas.

1.2 Finalidad práctica: la clasificación permite al usuario describir una avalancha observada o esperada, utilizando términos simples, de fácil comprensión para cualquier persona familiarizada con el tema. La previsión o alarma sobre avalanchas, las operaciones de rescate y las obras de ingeniería se ven así facilitadas por el lenguaje común que ofrece la clasificación.

1.3 El código empleado para la clasificación morfológica (sección 2.3) proporciona una representación abreviada y es particularmente útil para el registro y la transmisión de observaciones.

1.4 Esquema general de la clasificación: los rasgos y condiciones genéticas de una avalancha se subdividen de la siguiente forma:

	Características descriptivas (cualitativas)
	Tipos de avalanchas
Fenómeno inmediato de la avalancha	*Clasificación morfológica*
	Características mensurables (cuantitativas)
	Efectos de la avalancha (daños, víctimas)
	Condiciones del terreno
	Estratificación de la cobertura de nieve
Condiciones genéticas de la formación de la avalancha	Factores meteorológicos (anteriores y actuales)
	Mecanismo de activación
	Clasificación genética (clasificación de las condiciones de la avalancha)

Entre los rasgos inmediatos de la avalancha y las condiciones genéticas, existe una estrecha interrelación. Por ejemplo, en ambos se incluyen las condiciones del terreno. En este ejercicio, no se abordan con detalle las características mensurables y los efectos de la avalancha. Se pone el acento en la clasificación morfológica. En cuanto a la clasificación genética, se facilita un esquema provisional para las relaciones más importantes que han sido corroboradas.

2   Clasificación morfológica de avalanchas

2.1   *Esquema de clasificación*

Zona	Criterio	Características, alternativas, denominaciones y código	
Zona de inicio	A Forma de iniciación	A1 iniciación desde un punto (avalancha de nieve suelta)	A2 iniciación desde una línea (avalancha de placa) A3 blanda A4 dura
	B Posición de la superficie de deslizamiento	B1 dentro del manto nivoso (avalancha de la capa de superficie) B2 fractura de nieve nueva B3 fractura de nieve ántigua	B4 sobre el suelo (avalancha en profundidad)
	C Agua líquida en la nieve	C1 ausente (avalancha de nieve seca)	C2 presente (avalancha de nieve húmeda)
Zona intermedia (flujo libre y retardado)	D Forma de la senda	D1 Senda en pendiente abierta (avalancha sin confinar)	D2 avalancha en hondonada o canal (avalancha acanalada)
	E Forma del movimiento	E1 nube de nieve en polvo (avalancha en polvo)	E2 discurriendo a lo largo del suelo (avalancha de flujo)
Zona de depositación	F Rugosidad superficial del depósito	F1 gruesa (depósito grueso) F2 bloques F3 fragmentos angulosos redondeados	F4 fina (depósito fino)
	G Agua líquida en los escombros de la nieve en el momento del depósito	G1 ausente (depósito de avalancha seca)	G2 presente (depósito de avalancha húmeda)
	H Contaminación del depósito	H1 sin contaminación aparente (avalancha limpia)	H2 contaminación presente (avalancha contaminada) H3 escombros H4 ramas, de roca, árboles tierra H5 escombros de estructuras

2.2   *Comentarios sobre la clasificación morfológica*

2.2.1   **Definición de las zonas**

Zona de inicio

Es la zona en que la aparición de una avalancha se caracteriza por la forma de iniciarse. Para una avalancha de placa comprende la distancia hasta la fractura debida a la presión; para una avalancha de nieve suelta no existe ningún límite inferior definido. En la mayoría de los casos, la zona de inicio comprende una distancia de unos 100 metros.

Zona intermedia

El flujo (o movimiento) es independiente de la forma de iniciación. La velocidad puede ser creciente, uniforme o decreciente. Una vez que ha pasado la avalancha, no queda visible ningún depósito de avalancha en particular, exceptuando la nieve retenida por la rugosidad del terreno (por ejemplo, en barrancos estrechos).

Zona de depositación

La pérdida de energía debida a la fricción produce un depósito natural. La zona de depositación puede presentar una amplia gama de ángulos de pendiente, incluso una pendiente invertida. La posición de su límite con la zona intermedia puede variar considerablemente entre una y otra avalancha en la misma senda, según la calidad de la nieve (seca, húmeda, densa, etc.). Para avalanchas en polvo, la zona de depositación es la zona de sedimentación de la nube de nieve.

2.2.2   **Criterios y características alternativas**

Generalidades

Para cada criterio se ofrecen dos características alternativas, de las cuales, algunas se subdividen en subcaracterísticas. Si no se utiliza la subdivisión (porque la discriminación no es posible o no se desea), se aplica el término común. En algunos casos, las características alternativas son mutuamente excluyentes; en otros, pueden observarse ambas. Frecuentemente, o no se observan todas las características o no interesan todas para un determinado problema. El sistema flexible permite utilizar solamente las pertinentes en la comunicación oral o escrita. Los términos que aparecen entre paréntesis son los que deben utilizarse (véanse las ilustraciones).

Las letras mayúsculas atribuidas a los criterios, combinadas con cifras para las características, pueden utilizarse como código para el registro y para la transmisión de datos (véase la sección 2.3).

Comentarios detallados:
A. Forma de iniciación

Avalancha de nieve suelta. El punto de iniciación puede ser activado por la caída de un objeto (piedra, pedazo grueso de hielo) o por un esquiador. En este último caso, el mecanismo de la fractura en dicho punto es poco claro.

Avalancha de placa. La «iniciación a partir de una línea» no excluye que el origen del movimiento se propague como una fractura invisible desde un punto de iniciación único. El término «placa» es utilizado con frecuencia como sinónimo de «avalancha de placa», pero debe evitarse a menos que no exista duda sobre el significado correcto.

Distinción entre placa blanda y dura: en una *placa blanda,* la capa de nieve rota es muy blanda o blanda (véase la clasificación de la nieve). La placa se desintegra en material suelto, inmediatamente después de la iniciación. En una *placa dura,* la capa de nieve rota es semidura, dura o muy dura. Los trozos o bloques angulosos de nieve son transportados durante una mayor o menor distancia según la rugosidad del camino recorrido por la avalancha. La fractura de la placa puede observarse sin que una avalancha se produzca ulteriormente (fenómeno relacionado frecuentemente con el movimiento deslizante lento de la nieve húmeda; véanse las figuras 63, 64). Debido a la intensa lubricación producida por el agua derretida, el deslizamiento de la nieve puede transformarse en movimiento de avalancha. Este proceso se describe mediante el término «avalancha de deslizamiento» (véase la figura 18).

B. *Posición de la superficie de deslizamiento*

Dentro del manto nivoso. La «nieve nueva» en la «fractura de nieve nueva» se define como una capa uniforme de nieve depositada más o menos continuamente dentro de los cinco días anteriores a la fecha de la avalancha y que no comprenda tipos de nieve granulares. Se presenta la fractura de nieve nueva aunque las condiciones de la superficie de la nieve antigua, que hay inmediatamente debajo, hayan favorecido la fractura (por ejemplo, escarcha superficial, superficie suelta, costra helada). La superficie deslizante de una «fractura de nieve antigua» se encuentra dentro de la nieve antigua (nieve de más de cinco días), contribuyendo así dicha nieve a la avalancha en la línea de la fractura. No importa el que la mayor parte de la nieve de las avalanchas esté formada por nieve nueva ni tampoco el que la carga de la nieve nueva sea la que haya causado la fractura.

Sobre el suelo. Deberá denominarse «avalancha en profundidad», aunque sobre el suelo quede un velo o algunas manchas de nieve debidas a la rugosidad del terreno.

C. *Agua líquida en la nieve al producirse la fractura*

Una «avalancha de nieve húmeda» requiere que se presente agua líquida a través de la capa de la avalancha, ya que de lo contrario la avalancha sería «seca» o «mezclada». La distinción puede resultar difícil si no se consideran las condiciones meteorológicas (temperatura, radiación, lluvia). El término clásico «avalancha de tierra», utilizado anteriormente bien para la «avalancha de nieve húmeda», bien para la «avalancha en profundidad», se reserva ahora a los fuertes y húmedos aludes de primavera que arrastran consigo rocas y material del suelo.

D. *Forma de la senda*

Muchas avalanchas acanaladas se inician como avalanchas sin confinar y solamente se concentran en uno o varios canales en la parte inferior de su curso. Si la fracción más importante está canalizada (la zona de fractura tiene frecuentemente forma de embudo), se caracterizan como «acanaladas»; en caso contrario, se notifica un tipo mixto, describiendo las secciones confinadas y acanaladas.

El *perfil longitudinal* de la senda de una avalancha es frecuentemente muy importante (variaciones en el ángulo de la pendiente, escalones intermitentes, formación de cascada). Una descripción cuantitativa del perfil puede evaluarse mejor que una clasificación complicada de todos los posibles perfiles del terreno.

E. Forma de movimiento

No se hace distinción alguna entre un movimiento deslizante de traslación ($v > \sim$ 1 *m/s*) y un movimiento flotante, desmoronante o rodante. En la zona de inicio, el movimiento sigue siempre el terreno (avalancha de flujo).

Muy frecuentemente se observan tipos mezclados. Las «avalanchas en polvo y de flujo mezclados», la «avalancha de flujo con componente de polvo», la «avalancha en polvo con componente de flujo» constituyen formas posibles de caracterizar los tipos mezclados. Un movimiento desprendido del suelo, bien en forma de tipo polvo o flotante, puede denominarse «cascada».

El *deslizamiento* y la *reptación* de nieve con bajas velocidades y efectos dinámicos insignificantes ($v < 1$ *cm/s*) no se clasifican como movimientos de avalancha (figuras 62–66).

F. Rugosidad superficial del depósito

Un depósito se considera como *grueso* si la dimensión media de los fragmentos es mayor de unos *30 cm*; en caso contrario es *fino*. Los bloques angulosos son fragmentos de depósitos de nieve original, caracterizando así principalmente la fractura de la placa dura. Los fragmentos redondeados incluyen también trozos de hielo irregulares.

G. Agua líquida en los escombros de nieve

Las grandes avalanchas secas en la zona de origen pueden recoger nieve húmeda en partes más bajas de la senda y cambiar su carácter. La nieve húmeda en los desechos o escombros causa depósitos duros y sólidos, casi impermeables al aire, circunstancia importante para los trabajos de rescate y para remover las avalanchas.

H. Contaminación de los depósitos

Son frecuentes los depósitos con zonas limpias y contaminadas independientes, en cuyo caso deben clasificarse como «mixtos». Además de una contaminación visible, las avalanchas pueden contener mezcla de materias extrañas casi invisibles o totalmente invisibles (polvo, partículas orgánicas, sustancias radioactivas, etc.). Éstas no se incluyen en la clasificación. Existen depósitos con una fracción altamente dominante de escombros (roca, tierra). Si tales depósitos son causados por deslizamientos de tierra o por inundaciones, no se clasificarán como depósitos de avalanchas, aunque contengan nieve.

2.3　*Código para la clasificación morfológica*

2.3.1　Generalidades

Símbolo para los criterios: letra mayúscula. Símbolo para las características: cifra. Uso general de las cifras: desconocido, no necesario o no aplicable 0; características específicas puras 1–6; características mixtas 7 u 8; referencia a observaciones especiales fuera del sistema del código, 9. Ejemplo de aplicación del código *en forma tabulada:*

A	B	C	D	E	F	G	H	J	Observaciones:
3	9	0	7	0	0	0	4	0	B9: 3 niveles de fractura

En forma resumida, refiriéndose únicamente a criterios seleccionados: D7, A3, H4, B9 (B9: 3 niveles de fractura). Cada grupo consta de una letra seguida de una cifra; el orden de los grupos no es esencial.

2.3.2　Código para la clasificación morfológica

Criterios	Símbolos		
Características	Criterios	Características	
		puras	mixtas
Forma de iniciación	A		
Avalancha de nieve suelta		1 ⎫	
Avalancha de placa (general)		2 ⎬ 7	
Avalancha de placa blanda		3	
Avalancha de placa dura		4	
Posición de la superficie de deslizamiento	B		
Avalancha de la capa superficial (en general)		1	
Capa superficial media, fractura de nieve nueva		2 ⎫ 8 ⎫	
Capa superficial media, fractura de nieve antigua		3 ⎬ ⎬ 7	
Fractura en profundidad		4 ⎭	
Agua líquida en la nieve al producirse la fractura	C		
Avalancha de nieve seca		1 ⎫ 7	
Avalancha de nieve húmeda		2 ⎭	
Forma de la senda	D		
Avalancha sin confinar		1 ⎫ 7	
Avalancha acanalada		2 ⎭	
Forma de movimiento	E		
Avalancha en polvo (dominante)		1 ⎫ 7	
Avalancha de flujo (dominante)		2 ⎭	
Rugosidad superficial del depósito	F		
Depósito grueso (en general)		1 ⎫	
Depósito grueso, bloques angulosos		2 ⎬ 7	
Depósito grueso, fragmentos redondeados		3	
Depósito fino		4 ⎭	
Agua líquida en el depósito	G		
Depósito seco		1 ⎫ 7	
Depósito húmedo		2 ⎭	

Criterios	Símbolos		
Características	Criterios	Características	
		puras	mixtas
Contaminación del depósito	H		
Depósito limpio		1	
Depósito contaminado (en general)		2	7
Contaminado por roca, escombro, suelo		3	
Contaminado por ramas, árboles		4	8
Contaminado por restos de estructuras		5	
Mecanismo de activación[1]	J		
Activación natural		1	
Activación artificial (en general)		2	
Activación artificial, accidental		3	
Activación artificial, intencionada		4	

[1] Este criterio constituye un elemento de clasificación genética. Puesto que en la mayoría de los casos se conoce el modo de iniciarse la avalancha, dentro de determinadas alternativas, y es importante para algunos problemas, se añade al código morfológico.

3   Clasificación genética de avalanchas
(Clasificación de las condiciones de la avalancha)

3.1   *Generalidades*

En sentido estricto, una clasificación genética definiría una avalancha únicamente a partir de su origen. Pero, puesto que la mayoría de las avalanchas son el producto de varios factores genéticos de distinto carácter y de acción recíproca (por ejemplo, caída de nieve, viento y temperatura), una clasificación basada en un factor dominante por cada clase sería adecuada solamente para un número muy restringido de avalanchas, como, por ejemplo, avalanchas relacionadas solamente (o principalmente) con la caída de nieve nueva, con el viento, con elevadas temperaturas, con una deficiente estratificación. Por ello, se ha preferido adoptar otro punto de vista (del factor genético al efecto resultante de la avalancha), que consiste en compilar un catálogo de las condiciones de avalanchas y de sus efectos resultantes.

Un registro de las condiciones pertinentes de una avalancha observada permite un análisis genético y una explicación del acontecimiento; y, lo que es más importante, el estudio de estas condiciones hace posible evaluar el peligro antes de que se produzca la avalancha, y un estado de conocimiento avanzado sobre sus relaciones puede dar lugar a una *predicción* cuantitativa de las avalanchas (determinista o estadística).

3.2 *Clasificación de las condiciones de la avalancha*

Condición	Efectos sobre la actividad de la avalancha

A. Estructura fija

(1) *Condiciones del terreno*

(1.1) *Altitud relativa*

Situación topográfica general:	Dependiendo el efecto de la latitud y del nivel de las montañas circundantes.
—zona de crestas y de mesetas elevadas	Influencia de los fuertes vientos, cornisas, avalanchas de placas locales.
—zona por encima del límite arbóreo y por debajo de las crestas	Zonas extendidas de formación de avalanchas de placa.
—zona por debajo del límite arbóreo	Menor influencia del viento. Se reducen las avalanchas de placa; prevalecen las de tipo blando.

(1.2) *Inclinación* (ψ)

>35°	Es posible la formación de avalanchas de nieve suelta.
>25°	Es posible la formación de avalanchas de placa.
>15°	Flujo uniforme o acelerado.
<20°	Flujo o depósito retardados (avalancha fangosa en ángulos muy bajos).

(1.3) *Orientación de la ladera*

—con relación al sol	En laderas sombreadas aumenta la formación de avalanchas de placa secas. En laderas soleadas aumenta la formación de avalanchas húmedas.
—con relación al viento	En laderas a sotavento, aumenta la acumulación de nieve desplazada, aumenta la formación de avalanchas de placa. En laderas a barlovento, sucede lo contrario.

(1.4) *Configuración del terreno*

—pendientes abiertas y uniformes	Avalanchas sin confinar.
—canales, embudos y cordilleras	Avalanchas acanaladas, concentradas y confinadas.
—variaciones de pendiente	Fractura de nieve suelta o en placas, en pendientes convexas.
—escalones	Avalanchas en polvo, formación de cascadas.

(1.5) *Rugosidad*

—terreno liso	Deslizamiento de nieve (sobre terreno húmedo), se favorece la formación de avalanchas en profundidad.
—obstáculos salientes (rocas, lomos transversales)	Avalancha de capa superficial por encima del nivel de la rugosidad.
—vegetación	Hierba: favorece el deslizamiento de la nieve y las avalanchas en profundidad. Arbustos: reducen la formación de avalanchas, si no están cubiertos de nieve. Bosques: impiden la formación de avalanchas, si son densos.

B. Variables genéticas

(2) *Condiciones meteorológicas recientes* (período aproximado de cinco días antes)

(2.1) *Caída de nieve*	Aumento de la carga. Aumenta la masa de baja estabilidad. *Factor de máxima importancia para la formación de avalanchas.*

Condición	Efectos sobre la actividad de la avalancha
—tipo de nieve nueva	Nieve esponjada: avalancha de nieve suelta. Nieve cohesiva: avalancha de placa.
—espesor de los incrementos diarios de nieve nueva	Aumenta la inestabilidad con el espesor de la nieve ($\psi > \sim 25°$). Fractura de nieve nueva o vieja.
—intensidad de la precipitación de nieve	Inestabilidad progresiva con mayor intensidad, facilita la fractura de nieve nueva, amplía el peligro en pendientes suaves.
(2.2) *Lluvia*	Facilita la avalancha de nieve suelta húmeda o la avalancha de placa blanda. Nieve mezclada y corrimientos de tierra.
(2.3) *Viento*	Dos efectos: aumenta el depósito de nieve local (véase 1.3) y aumenta la fragilidad de la nieve.
—dirección	Aumenta la formación de avalanchas de placa en las laderas a sotavento. Formación de cornisas.
—velocidad y duración	Favorece la formación de avalanchas de placa locales, si aumenta la velocidad y la duración.
(2.4) *Condiciones térmicas* Factores importantes: temperatura y agua libre contenida en la nieve	Efecto ambivalente sobre la resistencia y el esfuerzo, es decir, sobre la formación de avalanchas: El aumento de la temperatura de la nieve causa crisis, pero finalmente produce la estabilidad. El aumento del contenido de agua libre facilita la formación de avalanchas.
—temperatura del aire	Tiene efecto similar a todas las exposiciones.
—radiación solar	Efecto dominante sobre las laderas expuestas al sol.
—radiación térmica	Enfriamiento de la superficie de la nieve durante la noche y en la sombra; importante con cielo despejado. Se facilita la formación de la escarcha superficial y profunda (véase 3.2).
(3) *Condiciones de nieve antigua* Influencias integradas de las condiciones meteorológicas durante toda la estación de invierno.	
(3.1) *Espesor total de nieve*	No es un factor dominante para el peligro de avalanchas. Influye en la masa de avalancha en profundidad. Es importante para la compactación y el metamorfismo del manto nivoso. Avalancha de capa superficial (véase 1.5).
(3.2) *Estratificación*	
—secuencia de la resistencia	Estabilidad regulada por la capa con menor resistencia al esfuerzo.
—capa superficial	Desprendimiento (escarcha superficial), fragilidad, rugosidad importante para la ulterior caída de nieve.
—interior de la capa de nieve	Fracturas de nieve antigua causadas por *capas intermedias débiles* (superficies antiguas) y *escarcha profunda*.
(4) *Mecanismo de generación*	
(4.1) *Activación natural* —influencias internas —influencias externas (no humanas)	Avalancha natural. Avalancha espontánea. Avalancha activada en forma natural.
(4.2) *Activación artificial*	
—iniciador accidental —iniciador intencionado	—Avalancha accidental (iniciada) —Avalancha artificial (iniciada)

3.3   *Comentarios sobre las condiciones genéticas y sobre los efectos*

(1.1) Altitud relativa

El efecto de la altitud es muy complejo. Influye sobre la temperatura, la radiación, el viento, la precipitación, la duración del invierno, la vegetación, la topografía general. El efecto es relativo en la medida en que es variable con respecto a la latitud y región climática.

(1.2) Pendiente

Debido a la variable resistencia y fricción de la nieve existe una gran variación en la relación entre el ángulo de pendiente y las condiciones de iniciación y deslizamiento de las avalanchas. Las cifras facilitadas representan valores comunes de inclinación pero no los extremos. Frecuentemente, se originan avalanchas de placa importantes y peligrosas en el margen comprendido entre 35° y 40°. Hay una superposición de los valores que favorecen el flujo uniforme o acelerado y el flujo y deposición retardados.

(1.5) Rugosidad del terreno

El deslizamiento de la nieve puede provocar grandes fisuras en el manto nivoso sin que se originen avalanchas. En las técnicas de protección contra avalanchas, se utiliza una clasificación particular de la rugosidad, caracterizada por un «factor de deslizamiento» N.

(2) Meteorología reciente

Las avalanchas causadas por condiciones climatológicas recientes y que tienen lugar con nieve nueva han sido denominadas «avalanchas de acción directa» (Tipo B2). Las avalanchas que comprenden un desarrollo a largo plazo (metamorfismo) en el manto nivoso antiguo (véanse las condiciones de nieve antigua, estratificación 3.2) han sido denominadas «avalanchas de evolución» (Tipo B3 o B4).

(2.1) Espesor de la nieve nueva

La mayoría de las avalanchas catastróficas que afectan a las zonas pobladas y un alto porcentaje de las avalanchas que se producen en las zonas de deportes de invierno guardan relación con la *deposición de nieve nueva*. El espesor de la nieve nueva se utiliza como factor más importante en la previsión de avalanchas. Debe hacerse una distinción clara entre las sumas de las mediciones de nevada diaria (incrementos diarios de nieve recién caída), el espesor asentado de una capa de nieve nueva acumulada en varios días y el incremento del espesor total de nieve (tres cifras diferentes).

(2.3) Viento

La fragilidad de un depósito de nieve desplazada por el viento es causa de fracturas frágiles y de esfuerzos locales máximos. Como norma general, las propias cornisas no son los puntos más peligrosos para la fractura de placas. Indican las condiciones del viento dominante, pero la fractura se produce generalmente debajo de las cornisas. En determinadas regiones, se informa sobre un límite superior de influencia del viento. Las zonas más altas pueden verse privadas de nieve, como consecuencia de vientos sumamente fuertes, en un grado tal que se reduce allí la frecuencia de avalanchas.

(2.4, 3.2) Condiciones térmicas y estratificación

Las variaciones de temperatura de la nieve, tanto si son provocadas por flujos de calor sensible o latente, o por la radiación incidente o reflejada, tienen un efecto inmediato e irreversible sobre las propiedades mecánicas de la nieve. Además, el aumento de la densidad influye en la modalidad e intensidad del metamorfismo de la nieve, es decir, en la transformación de los cristales de la nieve tipo nuevo y plumoso a granos de nieve antigua redondeados o facetados. En la presencia de un fuerte gradiente de temperatura, se forma escarcha granular, ya sea en profundidad o en la misma superficie, que representa una estructura granular gruesa y quebradiza, de cohesión relativamente baja. En ausencia de un gradiente de temperatura, la nieve se transforma en un material cohesivo de granos redondeados más pequeños. Estos efectos secundarios irreversibles de la temperatura tienen una acción retardada sobre las condiciones de la avalancha. Juntamente con la caída de nieve y el viento, controlan la estratificación del manto nivoso y son causa de la formación de capas débiles y de capas resistentes. Un aumento de la temperatura de la nieve hasta la de fusión causa cambios profundos e irreversibles de sus propiedades mecánicas, principalmente una acusada disminución de la resistencia.

4   Estudio completo de avalanchas

Una investigación detallada de la avalancha requiere, más allá de la clasificación morfológica, una serie mínima de datos cuantitativos medidos. Esto es importante para analizar los accidentes de avalanchas, la preparación de cartas de avalanchas y la planificación de una protección contra ellas. Un estudio completo de una avalancha incluye tanto los factores morfológicos como las condiciones genéticas.

Lista de comprobación para un estudio completo de la avalancha

1 Notas sobre el estudio del terreno

Nombre de los observadores, fecha, condiciones meteorológicas.

2 Cartas, croquis, fotografías

En las cartas, se marca el perfil general de la avalancha o las avalanchas (escala 1:5000 a 1:50 000). Los croquis permiten anotar las dimensiones y las características particulares (escala 1:500 a 1:5000). Las fotografías tienen valor documental. Las aéreas son de gran utilidad (particularmente si incluyen la zona de inicio). Ya que la calidad de las fotografías únicamente puede comprobarse *a posteriori*, deberán efectuarse siempre croquis.

3 Notas sobre los datos de la avalancha[1]

Emplazamiento: región, comunidad, orientación de la montaña.
Altitud: zona de inicio y de depositación.
Fecha y hora del incidente.
Clasificación morfológica.
Dimensiones de la avalancha: anchura y longitud de la zona fracturada. Espesor o profundidad media (y local) de la capa fracturada. Longitud y anchura de la zona de transición. Dimensiones (incluido el espesor) del depósito de la avalancha (volumen). Dimensiones de la zona de corriente de aire.
Orientación y ángulo de la ladera: zona de inicio, zona intermedia, zona de depositación (perfil longitudinal total).
Características dinámicas: velocidad, efectos de la presión (véase el punto 5 más abajo).

4 Notas sobre las condiciones genéticas

Condiciones del terreno: rugosidad del terreno, vegetación, condiciones geológicas.
Meteorología reciente (aproximadamente hasta cinco días antes): precipitación, viento, temperatura.
Condiciones de la nieve antigua: estratificación (perfil de la nieve).
Mecanismo de activación: causas naturales, artificiales.

5 Daños

Casos de personas afectadas: número y nombre de personas involucradas (incluidos testigos presenciales): víctimas, personas desaparecidas, personas lesionadas y rescatadas ilesas. Circunstancias del accidente.
Daños estructurales: tipo, número de objetos, grado de destrucción.
Interrupción del tráfico: carreteras, vías de ferrocarril, líneas de transmisión.
Daños a bosques, pastizales, pérdidas de ganado.
Efecto de las medidas de protección.

6 Operaciones de rescate

Acción de los testigos. Organizaciones participantes, número de personas que prestaron ayuda. Logística, progreso y éxito de las operaciones. Localización de las víctimas (medios, profundidad, tiempo). Estado y tratamiento médico de las víctimas.

---

[1] En la medida en que no estén incluidos en las cartas y los croquis.

Clasificación de la nieve (resumen)

Bajo el título «Clasificación Internacional para la Nieve», el Comité Asociado sobre Mecánica del Suelo y de la Nieve, Consejo Nacional de Investigación, Ottawa, Canadá, publicó en 1954 el *Technical Memorandum n.° 31*, que contiene una clasificación completa de la nieve, adoptada por la Comisión Internacional de la Nieve y el Hielo (1952).

Únicamente se reproduce aquí (cuadros 1, 2 y 3) un resumen de esta clasificación relacionada con la nieve depositada. Permite al usuario registrar en forma gráfica, normalizada y por escrito, la estratificación de la nieve y las condiciones de la superficie de la nieve en relación con la generación de la avalancha. La figura 1 presenta un perfil de nieve, que utiliza ese sistema.

Los símbolos utilizados en esta clasificación no guardan relación con el código de la avalancha y deben utilizarse por separado. Para determinar cantidades se utilizan aquí varios símbolos.

CUADRO 1. Clasificación de la nieve depositada

Características	Símbolos	Subclasificación* a o 1	b, 2	c, 3	d, 4	e, 5	Observaciones
Forma del grano (véanse las figuras 48 a 53)	F	forma original / nieve nueva	parcialmente ramificada / nieve poco posada como fieltro	redondeada / nieve antigua	facetada	nervado, en forma de copa, escarcha en profundidad	Fc: círculo abierto opcional para metamorfismo por fusión. De izquierda a derecha: metamorfismo progresivo
Tamaño del grano: diámetro medio (mm)	D	<0,5 / muy fino	0,5-1 / fino	1-2 / mediano	2-4 / grueso	>4 / muy grueso	Se indicará solamente en mm
Agua libre (%)	W	seco	húmedo	mojado	muy mojado	saturado	Wb: nieve pegajosa; Wc: agua visible; Wd: rezumando agua; We: saturada
Resistencia (N/m²)	K						Escala para resistencia (o dureza), véase detalle. Lentes de hielo (capa)
Dureza	R	muy baja / muy blanda	baja / blanda	media / medio duro	alta / dura	muy alta / muy dura	
Densidad (kg/m³)	G, ϱ						Sólo valores de densidad
Temperatura de la nieve	T						Indicar la posición de la medida

* a elección letras, cifras o valores medidos

Escala comparativa aproximada de la resistencia y de la dureza

Observación, medida	a, muy baja	b, baja	c, mediana	d, alta	e, muy alta
Cohesión, K (kN/m²)	0-1	1-7,5	7,5-25	25-50	>50
Dureza de penetrómetro (ramsonda 4 cm ∅) R (N)	0-20	20-150	150-500	500-1000	>1000
Prueba manual (puede introducirse fácilmente en la nieve ≈ 30 N)	puño	4 dedos	1 dedo	lápiz	cuchillo

10 N ≈ 1 kp

CUADRO 2. Condiciones de la superficie de la nieve (ver las figuras 50 a 61)

Características	Símbolo	a, (1)	b, (2)	c, (3)	d, (4)	e, (5)
Deposición de superficie	V	escarcha superficial	cencellada blanda	cencellada dura	cencellada vitrificada	
Rugosidad de la superficie	S	lisa	ondulada	surcos cóncavos	surcos convexos	surcos casuales
Penetrabilidad (cm)	P	<0,5	0,5-2	2-10	10-30	>30

Profundidad de la penetración vertical (cm)   PS: Esquiador sobre un ski
PP: Hombre sobre un pie
PR: Primera sección de la ramsonda estándar

CUADRO 3. Símbolos para las mediciones de la cubierta de nieve

Características (m, cm)	Vertical	Perpendicular a pendiente	Inclinación de la pendiente (grados)	N, $\psi°$ (g)
Coordenada desde el suelo	H, h	M, m, D, d		
Profundidad total	HS, Hs	MS, Ms, DS, Ds	Zona específica cubierta por nieve (décimas)	Q
Caída diaria de nieve nueva	HN, Hn			
Equivalente de agua del manto nivoso (mm)	HW, Hw		Edad del depósito (horas, días, años)	A

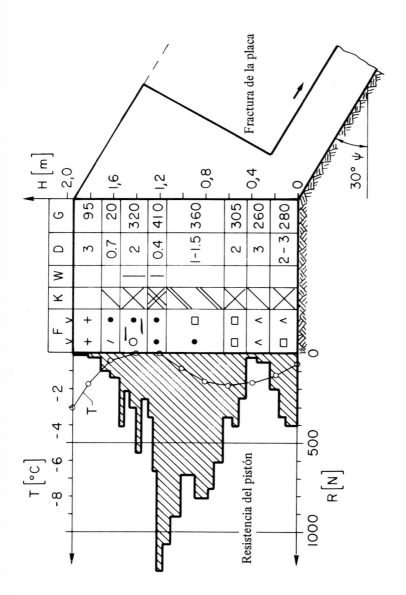

FIGURA 1. Representación de un perfil de nieve en una fractura de avalancha. (Para los símbolos y cifras, véase p. 74 y 75. Véase también la figura 49, un perfil de nieve por transparencia).

Международная классификация лавин

1 Принципы классификации лавин

1.1 Научные цели: сохранить наблюденные описательные характеристики лавин в сжатой форме, чтобы в дальнейшем получить статистические и детерминистские законы, управляющие лавинной деятельностью.

1.2 Практические задачи: классификация позволяет описать наблюденные и ожидаемые лавины наиболее простыми терминами, легко понимаемыми любыми другими людьми, которые ознакомились с системой. Лавинные предупреждения, спасательные операции, противолавинные мероприятия облегчаются использованием общего языка, предлагаемого классификацией.

1.3 Кодовые цифры позволяют сократить систему обозначений и облегчить передачу описывающих явление характеристик.

1.4 Общая схема классификации: явления формирующие лавины и лавинную деятельность подразделены в нижеследующей таблице:

	Описательные (качественные) характеристики
	Типы лавин
Собственно лавины	*Морфологическая классификация*
	Измеряемые (количественные) характеристики
	Воздействия лавин (разрушения, жертвы)
	Условия на подстилающей поверхности
	Стратиграфия снежного покрова
Генетические условия формирования лавин	Погода (предшествующая и настоящая)
	Причины схода лавин
	Генетическая классификация (классификация условий возникновения лавин)

Между собственно лавинными явлениями и условиями зарождения лавин существует тесная взаимосвязь. Например, условия на подстилающей поверхности влияют на оба процесса. В настоящее время обработка измеряемых характеристик и последствий воздействия лавин недостаточно детальна. Поэтому, особое значение придается морфологической классификации. В генетической классификации сделана попытка дать схему для наиболее важных и подтвержденных корреляций.

2 Морфологическая классификация лавин

2.1 *Схема классификации*

Зоны	Критерий		Альтернативные характеристики, их наименования и код	
Зона зарождения	A	Тип начала движения	A1 Двинулась из точки (лавина из рыхлого снега)	A2 Двинулась с линии (лавина из снежной доски)
				A3 Мягкая A4 Твердая доска доска
	B	Положение поверхности скольжения	B1 внутри снежного покрова (лавина поверхностного слоя)	B4 по грунту (лавина полной глубины)
			B2 срыв в B3 срыв в новом старом снежном снежном покрове покрове	
	C	Жидкая вода в снегу	C1 отсутствует (сухая лавина)	C2 имеется (мокрая лавина)
Зона транзита (свободное и замедленное течение)	D	Форма пути	D1 Движение на ровном склоне (неограниченная лавина)	D2 Движение в лотке (лотковая лавина)
	E	Тип движения	E1 облако снежной пыли (пылевая лавина)	E2 течение вдоль поверхности грунта (текучая лавина)
Зона отложения	F	Поверхностная шероховатость отложений	F1 Крупнокомковатые (крупнокомковатые отложения)	F4 Мелкокомковатые (мелкокомковатые отложения)
			F2 угловатые блоки	F3 окатанные комья
	G	Жидкая вода в снежных отложениях во время остановки	G1 отсутствует (сухие лавинные отложения)	G2 имеется (мокрые лавинные отложения)

Зоны	Критерий	Альтернативные характеристики их наименования и код		
	H Загрязнение отложений	H1 нет ясного загрязнения (чистая лавина)	H2 имеется загрязнение (загрязненная лавина)	
			H3 скальные обломки, остатки почвы	H4 ветки, деревья
			H5 обломки сооружений	

2.2   Пояснения к морфологической классификации

2.2.1   Определение зон

Зона зарождения

Зона, в которой появление лавин характеризуется типом начала движения. Для лавин из снежной доски она охватывает расстояние от гребня вниз до трещин сжатия, для лавин из рыхлого снега нет определенного нижнего предела. Расстояние в 100 метров в большинстве случаев обычно перекрывает зону зарождения.

Зона транзита

Течение лавины не зависит от типа начала движения. Скорость может быть возрастающей, постоянной или уменьшающейся. Обычно не отмечается никаких лавинных отложений после прохода лавин, за исключением снега, задержавшегося в неровностях рельефа (например, в узких врезах).

Зона отложения

Отложения снега появляются в результате потери энергии на преодоление сил трения. Зона отложения может лежать на склонах с различными углами наклона, включая противоположные склоны. Границы этой зоны, особенно границы с зоной транзита, могут лежать на разной высоте, в зависимости от типа лавинного снега (сухой, мокрый, плотный и т.д.). Для пылевых лавин зона отложений есть зона отложений снежного облака.

2.2.2   Критерии и альтернативные характеристики

Для каждого критерия предложены 2 альтернативные характеристики, которые в некоторых случаях подразделены на подхарактеристики. Если нет подразделения (разделение невозможно или нежелательно) используются общие характеристики. В некоторых случаях альтернативние характеристики исключают друг друга, в других случаях они могут существовать совместно. Часто не все характеристики наблюдаются или не все они интересны для определенной задачи. Гибкая классификация позволяет использовать только необходимые характеристики для устных или письменных сообщений.

Термины, данные в скобках, также необходимо использовать (см. иллюстрации). Заглавные буквы, используемые в критериях и комбинируемые с цифрами для характеристик, могут быть использованы как код для системы записи и передачи данных (см. 2.3).

Подробные комментарии
А. Тип начала движения

Лавины из рыхлого снега: могут образоваться в результате падения какого-нибудь предмета (камня, куска льда и т.д.) или быть вызваны лыжником. В последнем случае механизм начала движения из «точки» затушевывается.

Лавины из снежной доски: начало движения с линии отрыва не исключает, что оно было вызвано трещиной, которая тянется от невидимой отдаленной точки, где была причина, вызвавшая разрыв. Термин «доска» часто используется в английском языке как синоним термина лавина, чего необходимо избегать в случаях, когда не известен механизм начала движения и тип снега. Различие между мягкими и твердыми досками: *мягкие доски:* взломанный снежный покров очень мягкий или мягкий (см. Классификацию снега). Доска рассыпается, образуя рыхлый материал, немедленно после начала движения. Твердые доски: взломанный снежный покров средней твердости, твердый или очень твердый; куски и угловатые блоки снега долго сохраняются в процессе движения. Линии разрыва могут наблюдаться в снегу и без сопутствующих лавин (обычно это происходит в результате медленного сползания мокрого снега. см. иллюстрации 68, 69). Однако в результате сильного промачивания тающей водой медленное сползание снега может привести к образованию лавины. Этот процесс обычно описывается термином «скользящая лавина» (см. иллюстрацию 18).

В. Положение поверхности скольжения

Внутри снежного покрова: «новый снег», находящийся на «поверхности срыва в новом снежном покрове», определяется как однородный слой снега более или менее непрерывно отлагавшийся в течение 5 дней, предшествующих сходу лавины, этот термин не применяется к гранулированным типам снега. Термин «срыв в новом снежном покрове» используется, даже если срыв произошел благодаря условиям, существовавшим на поверхности подстилающего слоя старого снега (т.е. при поверхностной изморози, разрыхленной поверхности, ледяной корке). «*Срыв в старом снежном покрове*» обычно происходит *внутри* старого снежного покрова, который определяется как снег, отложенный более пяти дней назад. Старый снег поступает в лавину с поверхности срыва. В дальнейшем неважно, состоит ли лавина из нового снега или она произошла в результате перегрузки склона новым снегом.

Срыв по поверхности земли: если на земле остается снежная пелена или отдельные пятна снега (из- за неровностей поверхности) все равно считается, что это «лавина полной глубины».

С. Жидкая вода в снегу при срыве лавины

Термин «мокрая снежная лавина» применяется только в случае, если жидкая вода присутствует во всем слое снега, формирующем лавину, в противном случае, лавина будет или смешанной, или сухой. Необходимо отметить, что определение этой характеристики затруднено без учета погоды, температуры, солнечной радиации, дождя. Классический термин «грунтовая лавина», который раньше использовался для мокрых лавин или для лавин полной глубины, сейчас зарезервирован только для тяжелых, мокрых весенних лавин, сдирающих и несущих обломки скал и почву.

D. Форма лавинного пути

Многие канализованные лавины начинаются на ровном склоне и затем ниже по склону концентрируются в одном или нескольких руслах. Если большую часть лавины представляет русло (лоток) (зона срыва часто имеет воронкообразную форму), то она характеризуется как «канализованная», лавина описывается как смешанная, если ее путь состоит из ровного склона и русловой части.

Продольный профиль пути лавины имеет большое значение для ее характеристики (изменение угла склона, перемежающиеся уступы, обрывы). Точный геодезический профиль пути лавины всегда лучше любой тщательно разработанной классификации профилей схода лавин.

E. Тип движения

Нет точного разделения между скольжением снега ($v > \sim 1$ м/сек.) и течением, осыпанием или качением. В зоне зарождения движение всегда происходит вдоль поверхности земли (текучие лавины).

Смешанные типы движения лавин наблюдаются очень часто. «Смешанная текучая и пылевая лавина», «текучая лавина с пылевой частью», «пылевая лавина с текучей частью» – все это возможные описания смешанного типа движения. Движение лавины, отделенное от земли – пылевой или текучего типа – может быть названо «каскадным».

Сползание и скольжение снега с малой скоростью и незначительными динамическими эффектами ($v < \sim 1$ м/сек.) не считается лавинным движением (см. иллюстрации 62–66).

F. Поверхностная шероховатость отложений

Отложения считаются крупнокомковатыми, если средний размер обломков больше, чем 30 см, остальные называются мелкокомковатыми. Угловатые блоки снега и остатки ненарушенного в процессе движения снежного покрова обычно характеризуют лавину из твердой снежной доски. Окатанные комья также включают и комья снега неправильной формы.

G. Жидкая вода в снежных отложениях

Большие лавины, сухие в зоне зарождения, могут на пути движения захватить мокрый снег в нижней части пути и тем самым изменить свои свойства. Мокрый снег образует в лавинном конусе твердые и плотные отложения, не проницаемые для воздуха, что является важным фактом при проведении спасательных работ и расчистке лавинных отложений.

H. Загрязнение отложений

Отложения с перемежающимися чистыми и загрязненными участками в лавинном конусе очень часты и классифицируются как смешанные. Кроме

Причины	Воздействие на лавинную активность
(3) *Условия в старом снежном покрове*	
Интегральное влияние предшествующих погодных условий за зимний сезон.	
(3.1) Общая высота снежного покрова	Не определяющий фактор лавинной опасности. Влияет на массу лавин полной глубины. Важна для уплотнения снега и развития процесса метаморфизма в нем. Поверхностные лавины (см. 1.5).
(3.2) *Стратиграфия*	
Распределение напряжений	Стабильность зависит от слабейшего слоя и распределения напряжений.
– поверхностный слой	Рыхлость (поверхностная изморозь), хрупкость, шероховатость – важны при последующих снегопадах.
– внутреннее состояние снежного покрова	Срывы в слое старого снега по ослабленным внутренним слоям (старая поверхность снега) и по слою глубинной изморози.
(4) *Причины схода лавин*	
(4.1) *Естественный сход лавин*	Естественные лавины.
– внутренние причины	Самопроизвольные лавины.
– внешние причины, не связанные с влиянием человека	Лавины, вызванные внешними природными факторами.
(4.2) *Искусственный сход лавин*	
– случайно вызванные	Случайные лавины.
– специально вызванные	Искусственные лавины.

3.3   *Пояснения к генетической классификации*

(1.1) Относительная высота

Эффект воздействия высоты очень сложен. С изменением высоты меняются: температура, солнечная радиация, ветер, осадки, продолжительность зимнего периода, растительность и характер рельефа. На все эти изменения накладывается еще и влияние широты и климатическое положение региона.

(1.2) Крутизна склона

В связи с большими вариациями напряжений и трения в снегу, в широких пределах изменяется крутизна склонов, на которых зарождаются и движутся лавины. Приведенные цифры представляют наиболее обычные углы наклонов склонов (без включения экстремальных углов), с которых сходят лавины. Большие и опасные лавины из снежных досок часто зарождаются на склонах с углом от 35 ° до 40 °. Существует частичное перекрытие между стационарным и ускоренным движением, а также замедленным движением и отложением снега.

(1.5) Шероховатость поверхности

Сползание снега может вызвать большие разрывы в снегу без схода лавин. В инженерных расчетах противолавинных мероприятий используется специальная классификация шероховатости поверхности грунта, которая характеризуется «фактором скольжения» N.

(2)   Текущая погода

Только лавины из нового снега, вызванные текущими погодными условиями, надо относить к лавинам «прямого действия» (тип B2). Лавины, возникшие в результате длительного развития старого снежного покрова (метаморфизма) (см. стратиграфия 3.2), называются лавинами «замедленного действия» (типы B3 и B4).

(2.1) Высота нового снежного покрова

Большинство катастрофических лавин, обрушивающихся на заселенные зоны, а также большой процент туристских лавин связаны с отложением нового снега. Его высота используется в предсказаниях лавин как наиболее важный фактор. Необходимо точно различать следующие параметры: количество снега, выпавшего за сутки (суточный прирост высоты снежного покрова), глубину, высоту снежного покрова, образовавшегося за несколько дней, и увеличение общей высоты всего снежного покрова (три разные цифры).

(2.3) Ветер

Хрупкость ветровых отложений снега приводит к местным пикам напряжения и хрупким разрывам. Как правило, снежные карнизы не являются наиболее опасными местами для отрыва досок. Они показывают превалирующее направление ветра, но разрывы обычно случаются ниже карнизов. Для некоторых районов имеются сведения о верхнем пределе влияния сильных ветров на распределение снега: снежный покров сносится в результате влияния сильных ветров, что приводит к уменьшению лавинной опасности.

(2.4) и (3.2) Температурные условия и стратиграфия

Изменения температуры снежной поверхности, вызванные внешним или скрытым теплом или приходящей и уходящей радиацией, имеют прямой и обратный эффект на механические свойства снега. Кроме того, изменения температуры влияют на уплотнение снега и ход и интенсивность метаморфических процессов, т. е. трансформацию снежных кристаллов от пушистых снежинок к округлым или ограненным старым снежным зернам. В условиях большого температурного градиента формируется глубинная изморозь (на поверхности – поверхностная изморозь), что приводит к появлению грубозернистых и хрупких структур, с относительно низкой связностью. Если температурный градиент отсутствует, образуется связный материал, состоящий из мелких округлых снежных зерен. Эти вторичные температурные эффекты имеют замедленное действие на зарождение лавин. Совместно со снегопадами и ветрами они определяют стратиграфию снежного покрова и ответственны за появление механически слабых и прочных слоев. Повышение температуры снега до 0 °С приводит к глубоким и необратимым изменениям механических свойств снежного покрова, особенно к резко выраженному понижению прочности.

4 Полное описание лавин

Детальные исследования лавин, кроме морфологической классификации, требуют хотя бы минимального набора количественных данных. Это важно для анализа лавинных катастроф, создания лавинных карт (кадастров) и планирования противолавинной защиты. Полное описание лавин включает сведения об их морфологии и генетических условиях возникновения.

Контрольный перечень полного описания лавины

1 Полевые записи

Фамилия наблюдателя, дата, погода.

2 Карты, схемы, фотографии

на картах показывается контур лавины (масштаб от 1:5000 до 1:50000). Схемы позволяют показывать точные размеры лавин и отдельные факты (масштаб от 1:500 до 1:5000). Фотографии являются ценным документом. Аэрофотоснимки особенно ценны (включающие зону зарождения лавин). Однако в связи с тем, что качество фотографии становится известно позже (после проявления пленки), необходимо всегда делать зарисовки и схемы.

3 Дополнения к документации лавин[1]

Местоположение: область, район, горный склон.
Абсолютная высота: зона зарождения и зона отложения снега.
Дата и время схода лавины.
Морфологическая классификация.
Размеры лавин: Ширина и длина площади отрыва. Средняя (и локальная) толщина оторвавшегося слоя. Обмеры (включая толщину) лавинного отложения (объем). Размеры зоны действия воздушной волны.
Ориентация и крутизна склона: зона зарождения, зона транзита и зона отложения (полный продольный профиль).
Динамические характеристики: Скорость, сила давления (см. (5), разрушения).

---

[1] Когда нет карт и схем.

4 Дополнения к генетическим факторам

Состояние поверхности земли: Шероховатость территории, растительность, геологические условия.
Текущая погода (до 5 дней назад): осадки, ветер, температура.
Состояние старого снежного покрова: стратиграфия.
Причины схода лавины: естественные, искусственные (вызванные людьми).

5 Ущерб, причиненный лавиной

Катастрофы с людьми: Число и имена людей, попавших в катастрофу (включая очевидцев). Погибшие, раненные и найденные невредимыми. Обстоятельства катастрофы.
Повреждения сооружений: Тип, число сооружений, степень разрушения.
Перерывы в движении: автодороги, железные дороги, подъемники.
Разрушения лесов, пастбищ, потери скота.
Работа противолавинных сооружений.

6 Спасательные операции

Действия очевидцев. Участие организаций. Количество оказывающих помощь. Тактика, развитие и успех спасательных операций. Местоположение жертв (способ, глубина, время). Состояние жертв, оказание медицинской помощи.

Классификация снега (выдержка)

Под названием «Международная классификация снега», полная классификация снега, принятая Международной комиссией по снегу и льду (1952 г.), была опубликована как технический меморандум № 31, Объединенным комитетом механики почв и снега, Национального исследовательского совета (Оттава), Канады в 1954 г.

Выдержка из классификации, относящаяся только к отложенному снегу, воспроизведена ниже. Эта классификация дает возможность наблюдателю записывать в стандартной письменной или графической форме стратиграфию снежного покрова и тип снежной поверхности, связанные со сходом лавин. Приводимые символы не связаны с лавинным кодом и должны быть использованы отдельно. Символы, состоящие из заглавных букв и цифр, предназначены для передачи по телетайпу.

Таблица 1. Снежный покров

Характеристика	Сим-вол	Подклассификация*					Замечания
		a или 1	b, 2	c, 3	d, 4	e, 5	
форма зерен (см. Рис. 48-53)	F	кристаллы свежий снег	частично видоизмененная структура войлокообразный	старый снег — округлые	ограненные	ребристые чашеобраз. глубинная изморозь	Fc - незамкнутые кружки используются для тающего метаморфизма. Слева направо развитие процесса метаморфизма в снеге
Размер зерен средний диаметр, мм	D	<0,5 очень мелкий	0,5-1 мелкий	1-2 средний	2-4 крупный	>4 очень крупный	Все цифры только в мм
Свободная вода, % от веса	W	сухой	влажный	мокрый	талый		Wb липкий снег, Wc вода, Wd вытекающая вода, We насыщенный водой
Прочность (N/M²)	K						
Твердость	R	очень низкая очень мягкий	низкая мягкий	средняя ср. твердости	высокая твердый	очень высокая очень твердый	шкалу прочности и твердости см. ниже
Объемный вес, кг/м³,	G, ҫ						только измерен. величины
Температура снега °C,	T						проставьте глубину измерений

* Произвольные буквы, фигуры или величины измерений

Приблизительная сравнительная шкала прочности (твердости)

Наблюденная, измеренная	a, очень низкая	b, низкая	c, средняя	d, высокая	e, очень высокая	
Сцепление (kN/m²)	0-1	1-7,5	7,5-25	25-50	>50	
Таранная твердость R (Пенетрометр 4 см ∅) RN	0-20	20-150	150-500	500-1000	>1000	
Упрощенный тест для твердости (предмет легко входит в снег) Сила 30 N	кулак	4 сложенных пальца	палец	заточенный карандаш	нож	10 N ≈ 1 kp

Таблица 2. Характеристики поверхности снега (см. Рис. 50–61)

Характеристики	a, (1)	b, (2)	c, (3)	d, (4)	e, (5)
Тип поверхностных отложений V	Изморозь (иней)	мягкий налет	твердый налет	гололед	неправильные борозды
Шероховатость поверхности S	ровная	волнистая	вогнутые борозды	выгнутые борозды	неправильные борозды
Податливость*, см. P	<0,5	0,5–2	2–10	10–30	>30

* Глубина вертикального проникновения в снег в см.

PS (лыжник на одной лыже)
PP (человек на одной ноге)
PR (первая секция стандартного пенетрометра)

Таблица 3. Символы измерения снежного покрова**

Символы измерения снежного покрова**

Характеристики, м, см	по вертикали	перпендикулярно к склону		
Координаты	H, h	M, m, D, d	Крутизна склона (градус, уклон)	N, $\psi°$ (g)
Общая глубина	HS, Hs	MS, Ms, DS, Ds	Отношение площади, занятой снежным покровом, к общей площади (в десятых)	Q
Глубина нового снега, выпавшего за сутки	HN, Hn			
Воый эквивалент снежного покрова (мм)	HW, Hw		Возраст отложений (часы, дни, годы)	A

** Для телетайпов и ЭВМ использовать только заглавные буквы.

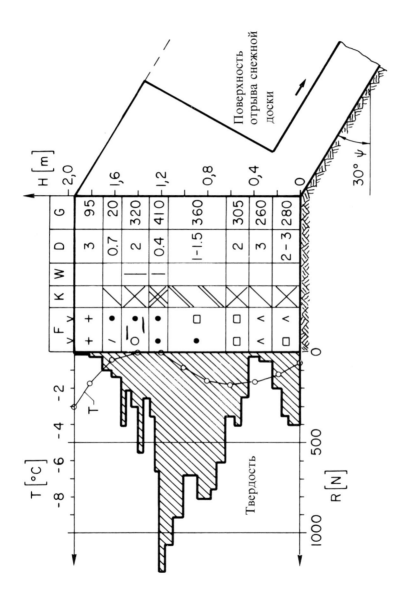

Рис.1. Пример профиля снежного покрова на линии отрыва лавины (символы и цифры см. предыдущие стр. 91–92).

Internationale Lawinenklassifikation

1 Grundsätze der Klassifikation

1.1 Wissenschaftlicher Zweck: Beobachtung und Beschreibung der Lawinenmerkmale in knapper Form, welche sich für die Erforschung der statistischen und physikalischen Gesetze des Lawinengeschehens eignet.

1.2 Praktischer Zweck: Die Klassifikation gestattet es dem Benutzer, eine beobachtete oder zu erwartende Lawine mit einfachen Begriffen zu beschreiben, die für Andere, in das System Eingeführte leicht verständlich sind. Lawinenwarnung, Rettungsaktionen, und bauliche Schutzmassnahmen werden durch die mit der Klassifikation eingeführte gemeinsame Sprache erleichtert.

1.3 Der Code für die morphologische Klassifikation (Abschnitt 2.3) ist eine abgekürzte Aufzeichnung und damit vor allem nützlich für die Aufnahme und Übermittlung von Beobachtungen.

1.4 Allgemeines Klassifikationsschema: die Merkmale einer Lawine und ihre Bildungsbedingungen werden wie folgt unterteilt:

	Beschreibende (qualitative) Merkmale
	Lawinenarten
Unmittelbare Erscheinungsform der Lawine	*Morphologische Klassifikation*
	Messbare (quantitative) Merkmale
	Lawinenwirkungen (Schäden, Opfer)
	Geländebedingungen
Bildungsbedingungen der Lawine	Aufbau (Schichtung) der Schneedecke
	Wetter (vorangegangenes und gegenwärtiges)
	Auslösebedingungen
	Genetische Lawinenklassifikation (Klassifikation der Bildungsbedingungen)

Zwischen den unmittelbaren Erscheinungsformen und den Bildungsbedingungen herrschen enge Beziehungen. Die Geländebedingungen beispielsweise sind in beiden einbezogen. In der vorliegenden Darstellung werden die messbaren Lawineneigenschaften und die Lawinenwirkungen nicht ausführlich behandelt. Das Hauptgewicht liegt auf der Morphologischen Klassifikation. In Bezug auf die genetische Klassifikation wird versuchsweise ein Schema der wichtigsten und bestgesicherten Beziehungen gegeben.

2 Morphologische Lawinenklassifikation

2.1 *Schema der Klassifikation*

Zone	Kriterium	Alternative Merkmale, Bezeichnungen und Code	
Anrissgebiet	A Anrissmerkmale	A1 von einem Punkt anreissend (Lockerschneelawine)	A2 von einer Linie anreissend (Schneebrettlawine) A3 weich A4 hart
	B Lage der Gleitfläche	B1 innerhalb der Schneedecke (Oberlawine) B2 Neuschnee- B3 Altbruch schneebruch	B4 auf der Bodenoberfläche (Bodenlawine)
	C Flüssiges Wasser im Schnee	C1 fehlend (trocken) (Trockenschneelawine)	C2 vorhanden (nass) (Nasschneelawine)
Sturzbahn (Durchgangsgebiet)	D Form der Sturzbahn	D1 flächige Sturzbahn (Flächenlawine)	D2 runsenförmige Sturzbahn (Runsenlawine)
	E Form der Bewegung	E1 stiebend als Schneewolke (Staublawine)	E2 fliessend, dem Boden folgend (Fliesslawine)
Ablagerungsgebiet	F Oberflächenrauhigkeit der Ablagerung	F1 grob (grobe Ablagerung) F2 kantige F3 runde Schollen Knollen	F4 fein (feine Ablagerung)
	G Flüssiges Wasser in Ablagerung	G1 fehlend (trocken) (Trockene Ablagerung)	G2 vorhanden (nass) (nasse (feuchte) Abl.)
	H Fremdmaterial in Ablagerung	H1 kein sichtbares Fremdmaterial (reine Ablagerung)	H2 Fremdmaterial sichtbar vorhanden (gemischte Ablagerung) H3 Steine, H4 Äste Erde Bäume H5 Trümmer von Bauten

2.2   *Erläuterungen zur morphologischen Klassifikation*

2.2.1   **Zur Definition der Zonen**

Anrissgebiet

Zone, innerhalb welcher die Erscheinung einer Lawine durch die Anrissform geprägt ist. Bei der Schneebrettlawine umfasst es die Fläche bis hinunter zum Stauchwall (Druckbruch). Bei der Lockerschneelawine kann keine scharfe Grenze angegeben werden. Eine Strecke von 100 m in der Fallinie wird in den meisten Fällen das Anrissgebiet einbeziehen.

Sturzbahn

Die Bewegung ist unabhängig von der Anrissform. Die Lawinengeschwindigkeit kann zunehmen, konstant bleiben oder abnehmen. Nach Durchgang der Lawine ist keine besondere Ablagerung sichtbar, ausgenommen ein durch die Bodenrauhigkeit bedingter Schneerückhalt (z.B. in engen Schluchten).

Ablagerungszone

Eine natürliche Ablagerung ergibt sich infolge Energieverlust durch Reibung. Die Ablagerungszone kann einen grossen Neigungsbereich umfassen, einschliesslich Gegenhänge. Gegenüber der Sturzbahn kann die Abgrenzung im gleichen Lawinenzug je nach der Schneequalität einer Lawine (trocken, nass, dicht etc.) sehr verschieden sein. Für Staublawinen gilt die Sedimentierungszone der Staubwolke als Ablagerungszone.

2.2.2   **Zu den Lawinenkriterien und Merkmalen**

Allgemeines

Für jedes Kriterium werden zwei alternative Merkmale unterschieden, die teilweise noch in Untermerkmale unterteilt sind. Wenn die Unterteilung nicht angewandt (nicht möglich oder nicht notwendig) wird, ist der obere allgemeine Begriff einzusetzen. In gewissen Fällen schliessen sich die alternativen Merkmale gegenseitig aus, in anderen können beide vorkommen. Häufig werden nicht alle Merkmale beobachtet, oder nicht alle sind für eine gegebene Fragestellung von Interesse. Das anpassungsfähige System gestattet es, im mündlichen oder schriftlichen Gebrauch nur die als wesentlich erachteten Merkmale einzusetzen. Die zu verwendenden Begriffe sind in Klammern beigefügt (Beispiele siehe Illustrationstexte). Die den Kriterien beigefügten grossen Buchstaben können zusammen mit den den Merkmalen zugeordneten Zahlen als Code für die Notierung und Übermittlung von Daten verwendet werden (Näheres siehe 2.3).

Einzelkommentare
A. Anrissmerkmale

Lockerschneelawine: Der punktförmige Anriss kann von einem fallenden Gegenstand (Stein, Eisstück etc.) oder durch einen Skifahrer ausgelöst sein. Im letzten Fall ist der Mechanismus des punktförmigen Anrisses nicht deutlich erkennbar.

Schneebrettlawine: Das Merkmale «von einer Linie anreissend» schliesst nicht aus, dass die Bewegung von einem unsichtbaren Anriss an einer entfernten Stelle ausgeht.

Der Begriff «Schneebrett» wird oft stellvertretend für «Schneebrettlawine» gebraucht. Dies ist zu vermeiden, es sei denn, der korrekte Sinn sei eindeutig erkennbar.

Unterscheidung zwischen weicher und harter Schneebrettlawine: *Weiche Schneebrettlawine:* Die angerissene Schneeschicht ist sehr weich oder weich (siehe Schneeklassifikation). Das weiche Schneebrett zerfällt sogleich nach dem Anriss in lockeres Material. *Harte Schneebrettlawine:* Die gebrochene Schneeschicht ist mittelhart, hart oder sehr hart. Schneebrocken oder kantige Schneeplatten bleiben je nach Bodenrauhigkeit über längere Strecken der Sturzbahn erhalten. Ein Schneebrettanriss kann ohne anschliessenden Lawinenniedergang beobachtet werden (oft in Verbindung mit der langsamen Gleitbewegung von Nasschnee) (siehe Fig. 63 und 64). Unter starker Schmierwirkung durch Schmelzwasser kann sich Schneegleiten zur Lawinenbewegung entwickeln. Man bezeichnet den Vorgang als «Gleitschneelawine» (siehe Fig. 18).

B. Lage der Gleitfläche

Innerhalb der Schneedecke: Unter «Neuschnee» im «Neuschneebruch» versteht man eine oberflächliche Schneelage, die innerhalb der vorangegangenen 5 Tage mehr oder weniger kontinuierlich abgelagert wurde, und die keine körnigen Schneeformen enthält. Ein Neuschneebruch liegt auch vor, wenn die Oberflächenstruktur der unterliegenden Altschneeschicht den Bruch begünstigt hat (z.B. Oberflächenreif, lockere Oberflächenschicht, vereiste Oberfläche). Beim «Altschneebruch» liegt die Gleitfläche *innerhalb* des Altschnees (Schnee älter als etwa 5 Tage). Altschnee ist also von der Anrisslinie weg in die Lawine einbezogen. Ob die Lawine mehrheitlich aus Neuschnee besteht und durch die Neuschneelast ausgelöst wurde ist in diesem Zusammenhang unerheblich.

Auf dem Boden: Auch wenn auf der Anrissfläche wegen der Bodenrauhigkeit ein Schneeschleier oder einige Schneeflächen zurückbleiben, ist die Lawine als «Bodenlawine» zu bezeichnen.

C. Flüssiges Wasser im anreissenden Schnee

Eine «Nassschneelawine» erfordert die Anwesenheit von flüssigem Wasser in der gesamten abgleitenden Schneeschicht, andernfalls ist die Lawine «trocken» oder «gemischt». Die Unterscheidung kann ohne Berücksichtigung der Wetterbedingungen schwierig sein (Temperatur, Strahlung, Regen). Der klassische Begriff der *«Grundlawine»,* der früher auf die Nassschneelawine oder die Bodenlawine angewandt wurde, ist jetzt für schwere, nasse mit Fremdmaterial befrachtete Frühlingslawinen reserviert.

D. Form der Sturzbahn

Zahlreiche Runsenlawinen brechen als Flächenlawinen an und werden erst im Verlauf des Absturzes auf eine oder mehrere Runsen konzentriert. Wenn der überwiegende Teil der Bahn in einer Runse verläuft (die Anrisszone ist oft trichterförmig), werden sie als «Runsenlawinen» klassiert, andernfalls wird ein gemischter Typ für die gesamte Bahn vermerkt.

Das Längenprofil einer Sturzbahn ist oft bedeutsam (Gefällsänderungen, Zwischenstufen, Kaskadenbildung usw.). Eine direkte quantitative Beschreibung des Profils ist einer Klassifikation aller denkbarer Geländeprofile vorzuziehen.

E. Form der Bewegung

Es wird nicht unterschieden zwischen einer translatorischen, gleitenden Bewegung ($v > \sim 1$ m/s) und einer fliessenden, bröckelnden oder rollenden Bewegung. In der Anrisszone folgt die Bewegung immer dem Boden (Fliesslawine).

Mischformen von Fliess- und Staublawinen sind sehr häufig. Je nach dem dominierenden Merkmal spricht man von einer «Fliesslawine mit Staubanteil» oder einer «Staublawine mit Fliessanteil». Die vom Boden völlig abgelöste Bewegung einer Staub- oder Fliesslawine kann als *Kaskade* bezeichnet werden.

Kriech- und Gleitschneebewegungen von geringerer Geschwindigkeit und vernachlässigbarer dynamischer Wirkung ($v < 1$ cm/s) werden nicht als Lawinenbewegungen klassiert (siehe Fig. 62–66).

F. Oberflächenrauhigkeit der Ablagerung

Eine Ablagerung wird als *grob* bezeichnet, wenn die mittlere Abmessung der Schollen grösser als ca. *30 cm* ist, andernfalls ist sie *fein.*

«Kantige Schollen» sind Stücke der ursprünglichen Ablagerung und zeugen somit von einem meist harten Schneebrettanriss. *«Runde Knollen»* schliessen auch unregelmässige Schneebrocken ein.

G. Flüssiges Wasser in der Ablagerung

Grosse, im Anrissgebiet trockene Lawinen können weiter unten Nassschnee mitreissen und damit ihren Charakter ändern. Nassschneebeimischung führt zu harte und dichten, weitgehend luftundurchlässigen Ablagerungen. Für Rettungs- und Räumungsarbeiten ist dieser Umstand von grosser Bedeutung.

H. Fremdmaterial in der Ablagerung

Ablagerungen mit getrennten reinen und mit Fremdmaterial durchsetzten Zonen sind häufig und werden als «gemischt» klassiert. Neben sichtbarem Fremdmaterial können Lawinen nahezu oder gänzlich unsichtbare Beimengungen enthalten (Staub, organische Teilchen, radioaktive Stoffe etc.). Diese bleiben in der Klassifikation unberücksichtigt. Es gibt Ablagerungen mit einem stark überwiegenden Anteil an Fremdmaterial (Steine, Erde). Wenn sie durch Erdrutsche oder Wasserausbrüche verursacht sind, werden sie nicht als Lawinenablagerungen klassiert, auch wenn sie Schnee enthalten.

2.3   Code zur morphologischen Klassifikation

2.3.1   Allgemeines

Symbol für das Kriterium: grosser Buchstabe. Symbol für die Merkmale: Ziffer. Allgemeiner Gebrauch der Ziffern: Merkmal unbekannt, nicht zu bezeichnen, nicht anwendbar, 0; reine spezifische Merkmale, 1–6; gemischte Merkmale, 7 oder 8; Hinweis auf besondere Angaben ausserhalb des Code-Systems, 9. Beispiel in *Tabellenform:*

A	B	C	D	E	F	G	H	J	Bemerkungen:
3	9	0	7	0	0	0	4	0	B9: 3 Gleitflächenlagen

Ausserhalb eines vorbereiteten Formulars, bezogen auf ausgewählte Kriterien, z.B. D7, A3, H4, B9 (B9: 3 Gleitflächenlagen). Jeder Ziffer geht ein Buchstabe voraus. Reihenfolge der Gruppen belanglos.

2.3.2 Code-Schema der morphologischen Klassifikation

Kriterium (Gesichtspunkt)	Symbole		
Merkmale	Kriterium	Merkmal	
		rein	gemischt
Anrissmerkmale	A		
Lockerschneelawine		1	
Schneebrettlawine (allgemein)		2	7
Schneebrettlawine weich		3	
Schneebrettlawine hart		4	
Lage der Gleitfläche	B		
Oberlawine (allgemein)		1	
Oberlawine, Neuschneebruch		2	
Oberlawine, Altschneebruch		3	8 7
Bodenlawine		4	
Flüssiges Wasser im Schnee am Anriss	C		
Trockenschneelawine		1	
Nassschneelawine		2	7
Form der Sturzbahn	D		
Flächenlawine		1	
Runsenlawine		2	7
Form der Bewegung	E		
Staublawine (vorherrschend)		1	
Fliesslawine (vorherrschend)		2	7
Oberflächenrauhigkeit Ablagerung	F		
Grobe Ablagerung (allgemein)		1	
Grobe Ablagerung kantige Schollen		2	
Grobe Ablagerung runde Knollen		3	7
Feine Ablagerung		4	
Flüssiges Wasser in Ablagerung	G		
Trockene Ablagerung		1	
Nasse (feuchte) Ablagerung		2	7
Fremdmaterial in Ablagerung	H		
Reine Ablagerung		1	
Unreine Ablagerung (allgemein)		2	7
durchsetzt von Steinblöcken, Schutt, Erde		3	
durchsetzt von Ästen, Bäumen		4	8
durchsetzt von Trümmern von Bauten		5	
Art der Auslösung[1]	J		
Natürliche Auslösung		1	
Menschliche Auslösung (allgemein)		2	
Menschliche Auslösung, unbeabsichtigt		3	
Menschliche Auslösung, beabsichtigt		4	

[1] Dieses Kriterium ist Teil der genetischen Klassifikation. Da die Art der Auslösung innerhalb der gegebenen Alternativen in den meisten Fällen bekannt und für viele Probleme wichtig ist, wird es dem morphologischen Code beigefügt.

3   Genetische Lawinenklassifikation
(Klassifikation der Bildungsbedingungen)

3.1   *Allgemeines*

Eine eigentliche genetische Klassifikation würde eine Lawine nach ihrem genetischen Ursprung bezeichnen. Da aber die meisten Lawinen das Ergebnis verschiedener zusammenwirkender Ursachen sind, wie z.b. Schneefall, Wind, Temperatur, würde eine Klassifikation, die nur auf *eine* dominierende Ursache für jede Klasse abstellt, nur eine sehr beschränkte Zahl von Lawinen erfassen, wie zum Beispiel: Lawinen hervorgerufen ausschliesslich oder vorwiegend durch Neuschneefall, Wind, hohe Temperatur, schwache Schneeschichtung. Daher wurde vorgezogen, von der genetischen Ursache zur resultierenden Lawine blickend, eine Zusammenstellung der Bildungsbedingungen und ihrer Auswirkungen zu geben.

Die Aufzeichnung der massgebenden Bedingungen einer beobachteten Lawine gestattet es, ihre Entstehung zu analysieren und zu erklären. Wichtiger ist die Untersuchung dieser Bedingungen vor einem Lawinenniedergang als Grundlage für eine Beurteilung der Lawinengefahr und, in gewissen Fällen, für eine *quantitative* (deterministische oder statistische) *Lawinenprognose*.

3.2   *Klassifikation der Bildungsbedingungen*

Bedingung	Auswirkung auf die Lawinenaktivität

A. Ortsfeste Rahmenbedingungen

(1) *Geländebedingungen*

(1.1) *Relative Höhenlage*

Bedingung	Auswirkung auf die Lawinenaktivität
Allgemeine topographische Situation	Wirkung abhängig von der geogr. Breite und der Überhöhung durch umgebende Berge.
—Kammlagen und Hochflächen	Starker Windeinfluss, Wächten, örtliche Schneebrettlawinen.
—Lagen zwischen Waldgrenze und Kämmen	Ausgedehnte Gebiete der Bildung von Schneebrettlawinen.
—Lagen unterhalb Waldgrenze	Verminderter Windeinfluss. Verminderte Bildung von Schneebrettlawinen. Weiche Form vorherrschend.

(1.2) *Neigung (ψ)*

>35°	Bildung von Lockerschneelawinen möglich.
>25°	Bildung von Schneebrettlawinen möglich.
>15°	Stationäre oder beschleunigte Fliessbewegung.
<20°	Verzögerte Bewegung oder Ablagerung. (Schneematsch-Lawinen bei sehr geringer Neigung.)

(1.3) *Hangrichtung*

—relativ zur Sonne	An Schattenhängen verstärkte Bildung von trockenen Schneebrettlawinen. An Sonnenhängen verstärkte Bildung von Nassschneelawinen.
—relativ zum Wind	An Lee-Hängen (windabgekehrt) Treibschneeanhäufung. Verstärkte Bildung von Schneebrettlawinen, an Luv-Hängen (windzugekehrt) umgekehrt.

Bedingung	Auswirkung auf die Lawinenaktivität

(1.4) *Geländeformen*

—offene, ebenmässige Hänge · Flächenlawinen.
—Rinnen, Trichter, Rippen · Runsenlawinen, konzentrierte, seitlich begrenzte Lawinen.
—Gefällsänderungen · Schneebrett- oder Lockerschneelawinen an konvexen Hängen.
—Gefällstufen · Staublawinen, Kaskadenbildung.

(1.5) *Rauhigkeit*

—Glatter Boden · Schneegleiten (auf nassem Boden). Bodenlawinen begünstigt.
—Herausragende Hindernisse · Oberlawinen über Niveau der Rauhigkeit.
   (Felsen, Querrippen)
—Vegetation · Gras: Schneegleiten und Bodenlawinen begünstigt.
Gebüsch: Verminderung der Lawinen-Bildung, wenn nicht schneebedeckt.
Wald: Lawinen-Bildung verhindert, wenn dicht.

B. Genetische Variablen
   (Veränderliche Bedingungen)

(2) *Laufendes Wetter*
   (Periode $\sim$ 5 Tage zurück)

(2.1) *Schneefall* · Zunehmende Belastung, zunehmende Masse geringer Stabilität.
   Wichtigster Faktor der Lawinenbildung.

—Art des Neuschnees · Flaumiger Schnee: Lockerschneelawinen.
   Bindiger Schnee: Schneebrettlawinen.
—Täglicher Neuschneezuwachs · Zunehmende Instabilität mit Neuschneehöhe ($\psi > \sim 25°$). Neu- oder Altschneebruch.
—Intensität des Schneefalls · Mit höherer Intensität progressive Instabilität, Förderung des Neuschneebruchs, Ausweitung der Gefahr auf Hänge geringerer Neigung.

(2.2) *Regen* · Förderung nasser Lockerschneelawinen oder weicher Schneebrettlawinen. Gemischte Schnee- und Erdrutsche.

(2.3) *Wind* · Zwei Wirkungen:
   —örtlich erhöhte Schneeablagerung (s.1.3).
   —erhöhte Sprödigkeit des Schnees.
—Windrichtung · Verstärkte Bildung von Schneebrettlawinen an Lee-Hängen. Bildung von Wächten.
—Windgeschwindigkeit · Mit zunehmender Geschwindigkeit und Dauer örtliche Bildung und Dauer von Schneebrettlawinen erhöht.

(2.4) *Thermische Bedingungen*

Massgebende Bedingungen: · Ambivalente Wirkung auf Festigkeit und Spannung, d.h. auf
   Schneetemperatur, Lawinenbildung.
   Schneefeuchte · Erhöhung der Schneetemperatur verursacht Krise, aber schliesslich Stabilisierung.
Erhöhung der Feuchtigkeit fördert Lawinenbildung.
—Lufttemperatur · Ähnliche Wirkung in allen Hanglagen.
—Sonnenstrahlung · Vorherrschende Wirkung auf sonnenexponierte Hänge.
—Temperaturstrahlung · Abkühlung der Schneeoberfläche in der Nacht und im Schatten, bedeutsam bei wolkenlosem Himmel. Förderung der Bildung von Oberflächen- und Tiefenreif. (Siehe (3.2).)

Bedingung	Auswirkung auf die Lawinenaktivität

(3) *Altschneebedingungen*
Vergangene Wettereinflüsse über
den ganzen bisherigen Winter
integriert.

(3.1) *Gesamtschneehöhe*

Nicht vorherrschender Faktor für die Lawinengefahr. Mitbestimmend für Masse von Bodenlawinen. Wichtig für die Verfestigung und die Umwandlung der Schneedecke. Betr. Oberlawinen siehe (1.5).

(3.2) *Schichtung*

Festigkeitsprofil

Stabilität bestimmt durch schwächste Schicht bezüglich Spannungszustand.

—Oberflächenschicht

Lockerheit (Oberflächenreif), Sprödigkeit, Rauhigkeit wichtig für Haftung weiterer Ablagerungen.

—Innere Schichten

Altschneebruch verursacht durch *schwache Zwischenschichten* (alte Oberflächen) und *Schwimmschnee* (Tiefenreif).

(4) *Auslösebedingungen*

(4.1) *Natürliche Auslösung*
—innere Einflüsse
—äussere (nicht menschliche)
Einflüsse

Natürliche Lawine.
Spontane Lawine.
Natürlich ausgelöste Lawine.

(4.2) *Auslösung durch Menschen*

—unbeabsichtigte Auslösung
—beabsichtigte Auslösung

Unbeabsichtigte Lawine (Auslösung).
Künstlich ausgelöste Lawine.

3.3   *Bemerkungen zu den Bildungsbedingungen und ihren Auswirkungen*

(1.1) Relative Höhenlage

Der Höheneffekt ist sehr komplex. Er beruht auf der Höhenänderung von Temperatur, Strahlung, Wind, Niederschlag, Winterdauer, Vegetation und Topographie. Der Effekt ist relativ, insoweit als er sich mit der geographischen Breite und der Klimaregion verändert.

(1.2) Neigung

Wegen des weiten Bereichs der Festigkeit und Reibung von Schnee sind die Anriss- und Fliessbedingungen in einem weiten Bereich von der Neigung abhängig. Die gegebenen Zahlen entsprechen häufigen Beobachtungen und nicht Extremwerten. Grosse und gefährliche Schneebrettlawinen lösen sich oft im Neigungsbereich zwischen 35° und 40°. Die Neigungsbereiche für stationäre oder beschleunigte Fliessbewegung und verzögerte Bewegung oder Ablagerung überlappen sich.

(1.5) Bodenrauhigkeit

Das Schneegleiten kann die Öffnung grosser Spalten in der Schneedecke hervorrufen, ohne dass Lawinen niedergehen. Im Lawinenverbau wird die Bodenrauhigkeit durch einen «Gleitfaktor» N gekennzeichnet.

(2) Laufendes Wetter

Lawinen, die durch das gerade herrschende Wetter bedingt sind und die nur Neuschnee umfassen, sind «Direkt-Lawinen» (Typ B2) genannt worden. Solche, die auf einer längeren Entwicklung (Metamorphose) im Altschnee beruhen (siehe Altschneebedingungen, Schichtung (3.2)) werden etwa als «Klimax-Lawinen» bezeichnet. (Typ B3 oder B4).

(2.1) Neuschneehöhe

Die meisten Katastrophenlawinen in besiedelten Gebieten und ein hoher Prozentsatz der Wintersportlawinen stehen in Beziehung zur *Neuschneeablagerung.* Die Neuschneehöhe ist das wichtigste Element in der Lawinenwarnung. Zwischen der Summe täglicher Neuschneehöhen, der Höhe der in mehreren Tagen aufgebauten gesetzten Neuschneelage und dem Zuwachs der Gesamtschneehöhe muss klar unterschieden werden (drei verschiedene Zahlen).

(2.3) Wind

Die Sprödigkeit von Treibschneeablagerungen führt zu örtlichen Spannungsspitzen und zu sprödem Bruch. Wächten sind in der Regel nicht die gefährlichsten Stellen für Schneebrettanrisse. Sie zeigen die vorherrschende Windrichtung an, aber der Bruch ereignet sich gewöhnlich unter der Wächte. In gewissen Gegenden wird eine obere Grenze für den Windeinfluss beobachtet. Höhere Lagen können durch Wind dermassen von Schnee entblösst werden, dass die Lawinengefahr dort vermindert wird.

(2.4) und (3.2) Thermische Bedingungen und Schichtung

Temperaturschwankungen des Schnees, hervorgerufen durch fühlbare oder latente Wärme oder durch einfallende oder ausgesandte Strahlung, haben eine unmittelbare und umkehrbare Wirkung auf mechanische Schnee-Eigenschaften. Darüber hinaus beeinflussen sie die Verdichtung des Schnees und die Art und Intensität seiner Umwandlung, d.h. die Verwandlung der Schneekristalle von den verästelten Neuschneeformen zu den abgerundeten oder kantigen Altschneekörnern. Im Bereich eines starken Temperaturgefälls bildet sich *Schwimmschnee* (oder *Tiefenreif*), an der unmittelbaren Oberfläche auch *Oberflächenreif.* Diese Schneearten besitzen eine grobkörnige und spröde Struktur von verhältnismässig geringer Festigkeit (Kohäsion). In Abwesenheit eines Temperaturgefälls wird Schnee in ein bindiges Material von kleineren rundlichen Körnern umgewandelt. Diese sekundären Temperatureffekte wirken sich auf die Lawinenverhältnisse verzögert aus. Zusammen mit Schneefall und Wind bestimmen sie die Schichtung der Schneedecke und sind verantwortlich für schwache und starke Schichten. Ein Ansteigen der Schneetemperatur bis zum

Schmelzpunkt zieht tiefgreifende und irreversible Änderungen der mechanischen Schnee-Eigenschafen nach sich, in erster Linie einen erheblichen Festigkeitsabfall.

4   Vollständige Lawinenaufnahme

Zur detaillierten Untersuchung einer Lawine benötigt man über die morphologische Klassifikation hinaus ein Minimum an gemessenen quantitativen Angaben. Dies ist wichtig bei der Analyse von Lawinenunfällen, der Aufnahme von Lawinenkarten und der Planung von Schutzmassnahmen. Eine umfassende Darstellung eines Lawinenereignisses schliesst sowohl morphologische Tatsachen wie auch Bildungsbedingungen ein.

Kontroll-Liste für eine vollständige Lawinenaufnahme

1 Notizen über die Feldbegehung

Namen der Beobachter, Datum, Wetter.

2 Karten, Skizzen, Photographien

Auf Karten werden die allgemeinen Umrisse der Lawine(n) eingetragen (Masstab 1:5000 bis 1:50000). Skizzen gestatten die Eintragung von Abmessungen und besonderen Merkmalen (Masstab 1:500 bis 1:5000). Photographien haben Dokumentarwert. Luftaufnahmen (besonders einschliesslich Anrissgebiet) sind sehr wertvoll. Da die Qualität von Photographien erst nachträglich festgestellt werden kann, sollten immer Skizzen angefertigt werden.

3 Notizen über die Lawinenmerkmale[1]

Örtlichkeit: Region, Gemeinde, Berghang.
Höhenlage: Anrisszone, Ablagerungszone.
Datum und Zeit des Niedergangs.
Morphologische Klassierung.
Abmessungen der Lawine: Breite und Länge der Anrissfläche. Mittlere (und örtliche) Mächtigkeit oder Höhe der angerissenen Schicht. Länge und Breite der Sturzbahn. Abmessungen der Zone mit Luftdruckwirkungen.
Orientierung, Neigung des Hanges: Anrisszone, Sturzbahn, Ablagerungszone (gesamthaftes Längsprofil).
Dynamische Merkmale: Geschwindigkeit, Druckwirkungen (siehe auch (5), unten).

---

[1] Soweit nicht in Karten und Skizzen enthalten.

4 Notizen über die Bildungsbedingungen

Geländeverhältnisse: Rauhigkeit des Geländes, Vegetation, geologische Verhältnisse.
Wetterablauf: (∼5 Tage zurück): Niederschlag, Wind, Temperatur.
Altschneezustand: Schichtung (Schneeprofil).
Art der Auslösung: Natürlich, durch Menschen.

5 Schäden

Betroffene Personen: Anzahl und Namen der Beteiligten (einschl. Augenzeugen). Todesopfer, Vermisste, verletzte und unverletzte Personen. Umstände des Unfalls.
Schäden an Bauten: Art, Zahl der Objekte, Grad der Zerstörung.
Verkehrsunterbruch: Strassen, Bahnen, Übertragungsleitungen.
Schäden an Wäldern und Fluren, getötetes Vieh.
Bewährung von Lawinenverbauungen.

6 Rettungsaktionen

Verhalten von Beteiligten (Augenzeugen). Teilnehmende Organisationen. Zahl der Helfer, Organisation, Ablauf und Erfolg der Operationen. Auffinden der Verschütteten (Mittel, Tiefe, Zeit). Zustand der Aufgefundenen, ärztliche Behandlung.

Schneeklassifikation (Auszug)

Unter dem Titel «The International Classification for Snow» wurde eine durch die Internationale Kommission für Schnee und Eis (1952) angenommene gesamte Schneeklassifikation als Technisches Memorandum Nr. 31 durch das «Associate Committee on Soil and Snow Mechanics» des «National Research Council», Ottawa, Canada, publiziert (1954).

Ein Auszug dieser Klassifikation, der sich nur auf *abgelagerten Schnee* bezieht, ist nachfolgend wiedergegeben. Er gestattet es, dem Benützer die *Schnee-Schichtung* und die *Schneeoberflächenverhältnisse,* die mit der Lawinenbildung in Beziehung stehen, in einer standarisierten Form verbal oder graphisch darzustellen.

Die darin benutzten Symbole stehen nicht in Zusammenhang mit dem Lawinencode und sind getrennt zu verwenden. Für gewisse Grössen werden verschiedene Symbole verwendet.

TABELLE 1. Abgelagerter Schnee

Eigenschaft	Symbol	Unterklassifikation*					Bemerkungen
		a oder 1	b, 2	c, 3	d, 4	e, 5	
Kornform (siehe Fig. 48-a-f)	F	urspr. Form — Neuschnee	teilw. verzweigt. S. etwas gesetzt, filzig	gerundet	kantig	gerieft Hohlformen Tiefenreif Schwimmschnee	Fc: Offener Kreis für Schmelzumwandlung (fakultativ); von links nach rechts zunehmende Umwandlung
Korngrösse mittlerer Durchm. (mm)	D	<0,5 sehr fein	0,5-1 fein	1-2 mittel	2-4 grob	>4 sehr grob	Zahlen nur für mm verwenden
Freies Wasser (Feuchtigkeit) (%)	W	trocken	schwachfeucht	nass	sehr nass	Schneematsch	Wb : Schnee pappig Wc : Wasser sichtbar Wd : Wasser fliesst ab We : Wassergesättigt
Festigkeit (N/m²)	K	sehr schwach sehr weich	schwach weich	mittel mittelhart	hoch hart	sehr hoch sehr hart	Eislinsen / schichten; Festigkeits- und Härteskala siehe unten
Härte	R						
Dichte (kg/m³)	G, ς						Nur Zahlenwerte
Schneetemperatur (°C)	T						Lage der Messung angeben

* nach Wahl Buchstabe, Zahlsymbol oder gemessener Wert

Angenäherte vergleichbare Festigkeits- und Härteskala

Beobachtung, Messung	a, sehr schwach	b, schwach	c, mittel	d, hoch	e, sehr hoch	
Kohäsion K (kN/m²)	0-1	1-7,5	7,5-25	25-50	>50	
Rammwiderstand (Rammsonde 4 cm Ø) R (N)	0-20	20-150	150-500	500-1000	>1000	10 N ≈ 1 kp
Handtest: (Gegenstand kann mit mässiger Kraft (≈30 N) in den Schnee gestossen werden)	Faust	4 Finger	1 Finger	Bleistift	Messer	

TABELLE 2. Schneeoberflächenverhältnisse (siehe Fig. 50 bis 61)

Merkmal	Symbol	a, (1)	b, (2)	c, (3)	d, (4)	e, (5)
Oberflächenablagerung	V	Oberflächenreif	Rauhreif weich	Rauhreif hart	Oberflächeneis, Glatteis	
Oberflächenrauhigkeit	S	glatt	gewellt	konkav gefurcht	konvex gefurcht	unregelm. gefurcht
Eindringtiefe (cm)*	P	< 0,5	0,5-2	2-10	10-30	> 30

* Tiefe des vertikalen Einsinkens in cm: Skifahrer auf einem Ski PS
                                             Fussgänger auf einem Fuss PP
                                             Standard Rammsonde (1. Abschnitt) PR

TABELLE 3. Symbole für Messungen der Schneedecke

Merkmal (m, cm, mm)	lotrecht	senkrecht zum Hang		N, $\psi°$ (g)
Koordinate ab Boden	H, h	M, m, D, d	Hangneigung (grad, gon)	N, $\psi°$ (g)
Gesamtschneehöhe	HS, Hs	MS, Ms, DS, Ds	Spezifische schneebedeckte Fläche (zehntel)	Q
Tägliche Neuschneehöhe	HN, Hn			
Wasserwert der Schneedecke (mm)	HW, Hw		Alter der Ablagerung (Stunden, Tage, Jahre)	A

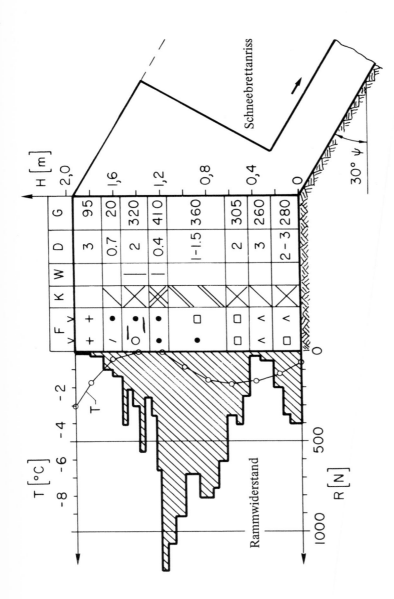

FIG. 1. Darstellung eines Schneeprofils aufgenommen bei einem Schneebrettanriss. (Symbole und Messungen siehe S. 108–109. Siehe auch Fig. 49, Durchscheinendes Schneeprofil.)

Photographic guide II

Guide photographique

Guía fotográfica

Иллюстрированное руководство

Photographischer Führer

General

The authorship of each photograph is indicated (name and country). Addresses are listed at the end of the atlas. The Eidgenössisches Institut für Schnee- und Lawinenforschung (Federal Institute for Snow and Avalanche Research), Weissfluhjoch/Davos, Switzerland, is indicated by the acronym EISLF. No further reproduction of the photographs is permitted. Request for information concerning the photographs should be addressed to EISLF. The location shown in a photograph is mentioned only if features of the surroundings can be recognized.

1 Morphological classification of avalanches (Figures 2–47)

Each photograph illustrates one criterion or characteristic. Other criteria are also mentioned to the extent that they are visible in the photograph or otherwise known. The index on page 121 lists all illustrated characteristics, based on the code.

2 Snow types and stratification (Figures 48–49)

Photographs showing the various metamorphic states of deposited snow.

3 Snow surface formations (Figures 50–61)

Influence of wind, temperature, radiation, vapour exchange on the snow surface.

4 Special formations (Figures 62–68)

Slow movements of snow cover (creep, glide, cracks, folds) and their consequences: drift deposits, cornices.

Remarques générales

La provenance de chaque photographie est indiquée (nom et pays). On trouvera en fin d'ouvrage une liste des adresses. Le sigle EISLF signifie Eidgenössisches Institut für Schnee- und Lawinenforschung (Institut fédéral pour l'étude de la neige et des avalanches), Weissfluhjoch/Davos, Suisse. La reproduction de ces photos est interdite. Toute information complémentaire sur ces photos peut être obtenue auprès de EISLF. La localisation d'une photographie n'est mentionnée que si le paysage avoisinant est bien reconnaissable.

1 Classification morphologique des avalanches (fig. 2–47)

Chaque photo représente un critère ou une caractéristique. D'autres critères sont aussi mentionnés, dans la mesure où ils sont visibles sur la photo ou connus par ailleurs. Le tableau de la page 121 constitue un index des caractéristiques codées illustrées par les photos.

2 Types de neige et stratification (fig. 48–49)

Photographies illustrant les stades de la métamorphose de la neige déposée.

3 Formations superficielles sur là neige (fig. 50–61)

Influence du vent, de la température, du rayonnement, des échanges de vapeur sur la surface de la neige.

4 Formations spéciales (fig. 62–68)

Mouvements lents du manteau neigeux (reptation, glissement, fissures, enroulements) et leurs conséquences: congères, corniches.

Observaciones generales

Se indica el autor de cada fotografía (nombre y país). Al final del Atlas aparece una lista de direcciones. EISLF es la abreviatura del Eidgenössisches Institut für Schnee- und Lawinenforschung (Instituto Federal para Investigación de Nieve y Avalanchas), Weissfluhjoch/Davos, Suiza. No se permite ninguna reproducción posterior de las láminas de este Atlas. Las solicitudes de información relativas a estas fotografías deben dirigirse al EISLF. La localización de una fotografía únicamente se menciona si pueden reconocerse las características del entorno.

1 Clasificación morfológica de las avalanchas (figuras 2–47)

Para cada criterio y para cada característica, se presenta por lo menos una fotografía. Todos los demás criterios se mencionan también en la medida en que resultan visibles en la fotografía o se conocen. El cuadro de la página 121 presenta un índice de todas las características codificadas e ilustradas por las fotos.

2 Tipos de nieve y estratificación (figuras 48–49)

Fotografías que ilustran los estados metamórficos de la nieve depositada.

3 Formaciones de nieve en la superficie (figuras 50–61)

Influencias del viento, temperatura, radiación, intercambio de vapor sobre la superficie de la nieve.

4 Formaciones especiales (figuras 62–68)

Movimientos lentos del manto nivoso (reptación, deslizamiento, grietas, pliegues) y sus consecuencias: deposiciones de acarreos, cornisas.

Общие замечания

Авторство каждой фотографии специально указано (фамилия и страна). Список адресов находится в конце. Сокращение EISLF означает Федеральный институт по исследованию снега и лавин, Вайсфлуйох, Давос, Швейцария. Право на воспроизведение фотографий было получено у владельцев. Дальнейшая репродукция воспрещена. Район съемки назван только в тех случаях, когда он может быть определен по окружению, показанному на фотографии.

1 Морфологическая классификация лавин (фото. 2–47)

А атласе даны фотографии для каждого критерия и характеристики. Все критерии наблюдались или были известны заранее.
Таблица на стр. 121 является указателем ко всем характеристикам, приведенным в атласе.

2 Типы снега и стратиграфия (фото. 48–49)

Фотографии стадий метаморфизма снежного покрова.

3 Поверхность снежного покрова (фото. 50–61)

Влияние ветра, температуры, радиации, испарения или сублимации на поверхности.

4 Особые образования (фото. 62–68)

– Медленные движения снежного покрова и его последствия (сползание, скольжение, трещины, складки)
– Метелевые отложения, карнизы.

Allgemeines

Die Urheberschaft jeder Photographie ist vermerkt (Name und Land). Eine Liste der Adressen findet sich am Ende des Atlas. EISLF bedeutet «Eidgenössisches Institut für Schnee- und Lawinenforschung, Weissfluhjoch/Davos». Eine Reproduktion der Photographien aus dem Atlas ist nicht gestattet. Anfragen um Information die Photographien betreffend sind an das EISLF zu richten. Die durch eine Photographie dargestellte Örtlichkeit ist nur bezeichnet, wenn Merkmale der Umgebung erkennbar sind.

1 Morphologische Lawinenklassifikation (Fig. 2–47)

Für jedes Kriterium und jedes Merkmal wird eine Photographie geboten. Alle weiteren Kriterien werden ebenfalls erwähnt soweit sie sichtbar oder anderweitig bekannt sind. Die Tabelle auf Seite 121 bildet eine auf dem Code beruhende Liste zu allen abgebildeten Merkmalen.

2 Schneearten und Schichtung (Fig. 48–49)

Abbildungen zu den Umwandlungsstadien von abgelagertem Schnee.

3 Bildungen der Schneeoberfläche (Fig. 50–61)

Einflüsse von Wind, Temperatur, Strahlung, Dampfaustausch auf die Schneeoberfläche.

4 Spezielle Bildungen (Fig. 62–68)

Langsame Bewegungen der Schneedecke und ihre Folgen (Kriechen, Gleiten, Spalten, Falten). Treibschneeablagerungen, Wächten.

1 Morphological classification of avalanches

Classification morphologique des avalanches

Clasificación morfológica de las avalanchas

Морфологическая классификация лавин

Morphologische Lawinen-klassifikation

Index to illustrated characteristics of the morphological avalanche classification (2.1, 2.3.2)

Index des caractéristiques codées et illustrées par les photos dans la classification morphologique des avalanches (2.1, 2.3.2)

Indice de las características codificadas e ilustradas de la clasificación morfológica de las avalanchas (2.1, 2.3.2)

Указатель иллюстраций к морфологической классификации лавин (2.1, 2.3.2)

Schlüssel für die abgebildeten Merkmale der morphologischen Lawinenklassifikation (2.1, 2.3.2)

	Fig. ИЛЛ.		Fig. ИЛЛ.
A1	2, 3, 4, 21, 22, 36, 43	E1	27, 28, 30
2	6, 12, 17, 18, 20, 23, 26, 33, 41, 43	2	2, 3, 4, 7, 12, 15, 17, 18, 19, 21, 22, 23, 24, 34, 35, 36, 37, 38, 39, 40, 41, 43, 44
3	8, 21, 29, 40	7	29, 31, 32, 33, 34
4	7, 9, 10, 14, 16, 19, (37)		
7	21		
B1	8, 9, 13, 23, 26, 28, 43	F1	17, 21, 24, 43
2	2, 3, 6, 21, 36, 40	2	7, 15, 37
3	4, 10, 12, 14	3	4, 19, 22, 33, 34, 38, 39, 41, 43
4	15, 16, 17, 18, 22	4	6, 21, 23, 36, 40
7	19	7	42
8	7, 21, 29		
C1	2, 3, 4, 6, 7, 8, 9, 10, 12, 13, 14, 15, 16, 17, 19, 21, 22, 23, 27, 28, 29, 30, 31, 32, 33, 36, 37, 45	G1	6, 7, 15, 17, 19, 21, 23, 33, 34, 36, 37, 38, 40, 42, 45
2	4, 18, 22, 34, 40, 41, 43	2	4, 22, 34, 38, 39, 41, 43, 44
		7	24
D1	2, 3, 4, 6, 7, 10, 12, 13, 15, 17, 18, 19, 20, 21, 22, 23, 28, 29, 30, 40, 48, 50	H1	4, 6, 7, 15, 17, 19, 21, 22, 23, 33, 34, 36, 37, 38, 40, 42, 43
2	24, 25, 27, 32, 33, 34, 38, 39, 41, 43, 44	2	39
7	26, 36	3	43
		4	51
		5	47
		7	24, 41
		8	44, 45

Morphological classification of avalanches
Classification morphologique des avalanches
Clasificación morfológica de las avalanchas
Морфо.югическая к.шссификация .швин
Morphologische Lawinenklassifikation

FIG. 2
Manner of starting:
Dry loose snow avalanches.
Other characteristics: Unconfined surface-
layer flow avalanches, evidence of earlier
cycle
Code: A1, B2, C1, D1, E2 or 1211 2000.
Location: Coal Bank Hill, Colorado,
United States.

Mode de départ:
Avalanches de neige sèche
sans cohésion.
Autres caractéristiques: Avalanches de
versant, superficielles, coulantes.
Deux périodes visibles.
Code: A1, B2, C1, D1, E2 ou 1211 2000.
Lieu: Coal Bank Hill, Colorado,
Etats-Unis d'Amérique.

Forma de iniciación:
Avalanchas de nieve suelta seca.
Otras características: avalanchas de flujo de
capa superficial sin confinar, evidencia de
ciclo anterior.
Código: A1, B2, C1, D1, E2 o 1211 2000.
Lugar: Coal Bank Hill, Colorado,
Estados Unidos.

Тип начала движения:
Сухая лавина из рыхлого снега.
Другие характеристики: Неканализован-
ные текучие лавины поверхностного слоя в
начальной стадии.
Код: A 1, B 2, C 1, D 1, E 2 или: 1211, 2000.
Район: Коал-Банк-Хил, Колорадо, США

Anrissmerkmale:
Trockene Lockerschneelawinen.
Weitere Merkmale: Flächenlawinen.
Oberlawinen, Fliesslawinen. Spuren einer
früheren Periode sichtbar.
Code: A1, B2, C1, D1, E2 oder 1211 2000.
Ort: Coal Bank Hill, Colorado, USA.

Photograph: E. R. LaChapelle, United States.

A. Manner of starting
A. Mode de départ
A. Forma de iniciación
A. Тип начала движения
A. Anrissmerkmale

Morphological classification of avalanches
Classification morphologique des avalanches
Clasificación morfológica de las avalanchas
Морфологическая классификация лавин
Morphologische Lawinenklassifikation

124

FIG. 3
Manner of starting:
Dry surface-layer loose snow avalanches.
Other characteristics: Unconfined flow
avalanches.
Code: A1, B2, C1, D1, E2 or 1211 2000.

Mode de départ:
Avalanches de neige sèche sans cohésion.
Autres caractéristiques: Avalanches de
versant, coulantes.
Code: A1, B2, C1, D1, E2 ou 1211 2000.

Forma de iniciación:
Avalanchas de nieve seca suelta de capa
superficial.
Otras características: avalanchas de flujo sin
confinar.
Código: A1, B2, C1, D1, E2 o 1211 2000.

Тип начала движения:
Сухая лавина поверхностного слоя из
рыхлого снега
Другие характеристики: Неканализованная
текучая лавина.
Код: A 1, B 2, C 1, D 1, E 2   Или: 1211 2000.

Anrissmerkmale:
Trockene Lockerschneelawinen,
Oberlawinen.
Weitere Merkmale: Flächenlawinen,
Fliesslawinen.
Code: A1, B2, C1, D1, E2 oder 1211 2000.

Photograph: M. Shoda, Japan.

A. Manner of starting
A. Mode de départ
A. Forma de iniciación
A. Тип начала движения
A. Anrissmerkmale

Morphological classification of avalanches
Classification morphologique des avalanches
Clasificación morfológica de las avalanchas
Морфологическая классификация лавин
Morphologische Lawinenklassifikation

126

FIG. 4
Manner of starting:
Wet surface-layer loose snow avalanches.
Other characteristics: Old-snow fractures,
unconfined flow avalanches with wet, clean,
coarse deposit. Traces of initial movement
visible.
Code: A1, B3, C2, D1, E2, F3, G2, H1
or 1321 2321.

Mode de départ:
Avalanches de neige humide sans cohésion,
superficielles.
Autres caractéristiques: Ruptures dans la
vieille neige, avalanches coulantes de versant
avec dépôt humide, propre, grossier.
Des traces du mouvement initial sont visibles.
Code: A1, B3, C2, D1, E2, F3, G2, H1
ou 1321 2321.

Formas de iniciación:
Avalanchas de nieve húmeda suelta de capa
superficial.
Otras características: avalanchas de flujo sin
confinar, con fracturas de nieve vieja, con
depósito húmedo, limpio y grueso. Hay
visibles indicios de movimiento inicial.
Código: A1, B3, C2, D1, E2, F3, G2, H1
o 1321 2321.

Тип начала движения:
Мокрая лавина поверхностного слоя из
рыхлого снега.
Другие характеристики: Поверхность
срыва лежит в старом снегу, Неканализованная текучая лавина с мокрыми,
чистыми крупнокомковатьми отложениями.
Хорошо видны пути первоначального
движения.
Код: А 1, В 3, С 2, D 1, Е 2, F 3, G 2, Н 1
Или: 1321 2321

Anrissmerkmale:
Nasse Lockerschneelawinen, Oberlawinen.
Weitere Merkmale: Altschneebruch,
Flächenlawinen, Fliesslawinen mit nasser,
sauberer, grober Ablagerung. Spuren der
auslösenden Bewegung sichtbar.
Code: A1, B3, C2, D1, E2, F3, G2, H1
oder 1321 2321.

Photograph: E. Wengi, EISLF.

A. Manner of starting
A. Mode de départ
A. Forma de iniciación
A. Тип начала движения
A. Anrissmerkmale

Morphological classification of avalanches
Classification morphologique des avalanches
Clasificación morfológica de las avalanchas
Морфологическая классификация лавин
Morphologische Lawinenklassifikation

128

FIG. 5
Manner of starting:
'Rolling snow'. Special type of 'avalanche',
occasionally triggering a loose-snow or slab
avalanche. Formation under wet new-snow
conditions. Diameter about 0.9 m.
(Not included in the classification scheme.)

Mode de départ:
«Neige roulante». Type spécial d'«avalanche»
qui peut fortuitement déclencher une avalanche de neige sans cohésion ou une avalanche de plaques. Se forme dans des conditions
de neige fraîche humide.
Diamètre 0,9 m environ.
(N'est pas compris dans le schéma de
classification.)

Forma de iniciación:
«Nieve rodante». Tipo especial de avalancha,
que activa ocasionalmente una avalancha de
placa o de nieve suelta. Formación en condiciones de nieve nueva y húmeda. Diámetro
aproximado 0,9 m. (No se incluyen en el
esquema de clasificación.)

Тип начала движения:
«Снежный камыш». Диаметр приблизи-
тельно 0,9 м.
Особый тип лавин, часто выступает как
причина схода лавин из рыхлого снега или
из снежных досок. Обычно формируется в
мокром новом снегу. (Не включено в схему
классификации).

Anrissmerkmale:
Schneerolle. Spezielle Art einer «Lawine»,
die gelegentlich eine Lockerschnee- oder
Schneebrettlawine auslöst. Entstehung bei
nassem Neuschnee. Durchmesser ca. 0,9 m
(nicht im Klassifikationsschema enthalten).

Photograph: R. Dorsaz, Switzerland.

A. *Manner of starting*
A. *Mode de départ*
A. *Forma de iniciación*
A. *Тип начала движения*
A. *Anrissmerkmale*

Morphological classification of avalanches 130
Classification morphologique des avalanches
Clasificación morfológica de las avalanchas
Морфологическая классификация лавин
Morphologische Lawinenklassifikation

FIG. 6
Manner of starting:
Dry surface-layer slab avalanche (new-snow fracture, artificially released).
Other characteristics: Unconfined flow avalanche with dry, clean, fine deposit.
Code: A2, B2, C1, D1, E2, F4, G1, H1, J4 or 2211 2411.

Mode de départ:
Avalanche de plaque superficielle sèche (rupture dans la neige fraîche, déclenchée artificiellement).
Autres caractéristiques: Avalanche coulante de versant avec dépôt sec, propre et fin.
Code: A2, B2, C1, D1, E2, F4, G1, H1, J4 ou 2211 2411.

Forma de iniciación:
Avalancha de placa de capa superficial seca (fractura de nieve nueva, iniciada artificialmente).
Otras características: avalancha de flujo sin confinar con depósito limpio, seco y fino.
Código: A2, B2, C1, D1, E2, F4, G1, H1, J4 o 2211 2411.

Тип начала движения:
Сухая лавина поверхностного слоя из снежной доски (поверхность срыва лежит в новом снегу, спущена искуственно)
Другие характерисики: Неканализованная текучая лавина с сухими, чистыми, мелкокомковатыми отложениями.
Код: A 2, B 2, C 1, D 1, E 2, F 4, G 1, H 1, J 4 Или: 2211 2411.

Anrissmerkmale:
Trockene Schneebrettlawine, Neuschnee-bruch, Oberlawine (künstlich ausgelöst).
Weitere Merkmale: Flächenlawine, Fliesslawine mit feiner, trockener, reiner Ablagerung.
Code: A2, B2, C1, D1, E2, F4, G1, H1, J4 oder 2211 2411 4.

Photograph: E. Wengi, EISLF.

A. Manner of starting
A. Mode de départ
A. Forma de iniciación
A. Тип начала движения
A. Anrissmerkmale

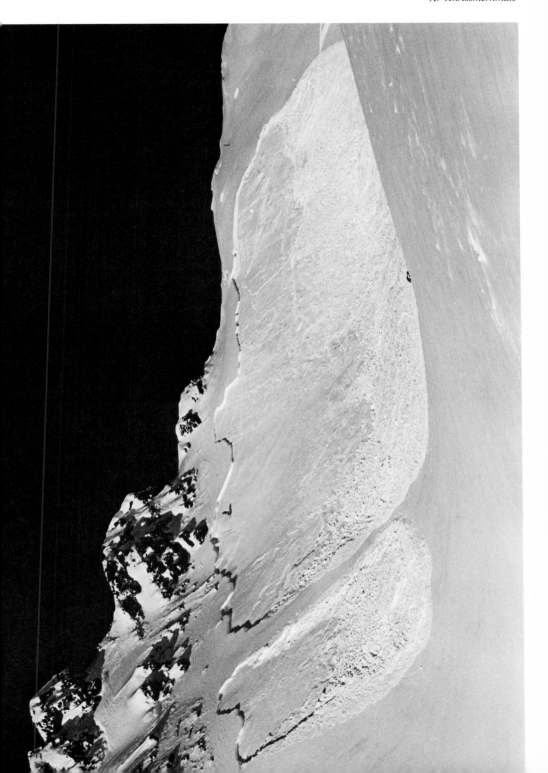

Morphological classification of avalanches
Classification morphologique des avalanches
Clasificación morfológica de las avalanchas
Морфологическая классификация лавин
Morphologische Lawinenklassifikation

132

FIG. 7
Manner of starting:
Hard dry slab avalanche.
Other characteristics: Unconfined surface-layer avalanche with mixed new-snow and old-snow fracture, flow avalanche, clean dry deposit with angular blocks.
Code: A4, B8, C1, D1, E2, F2, G1, H1 or 4811 2211.
Location: Alp Languard, Engadine, Switzerland.

Mode de départ:
Avalanche de plaque dure et sèche.
Autres caractéristiques: Avalanche superficielle de versant, avec rupture dans mélange de neige fraîche et vieille neige, avalanche coulante, dépôt propre et sec avec blocs anguleux.
Code: A4, B8, C1, D1, E2, F2, G1, H1 ou 4811 2211.
Lieu: Alpe Languard, Engadine, Suisse.

Forma de iniciación:
Avalancha de placa seca y dura.
Otras características: avalancha de capa superficial sin confinar, con fractura de nieve vieja y nieve nueva mezcladas, avalancha de flujo, depósito seco y limpio con bloques angulosos.
Código: A4, B8, C1, D1, E2, F2, G1, H1 o 4811 2211.
Lugar: Alp Languard, Engadine, Suiza.

Тип начала движения:
Сухая лавина поверхностного слоя из твердой снежной доски.
Другие характеристики: Неканализованная лавина поверхностного слоя с плоскостью срыва лежащей в новом и старом снегу, чистыми сухими отложениями из угловатых блоков.
Код: А 4, В 8, С 1, D 1, Е 2, F 2, G 1, H 1
Или: 4811 2211
Район: Альп-Ленгард, Энгадин, Швейцария

Anrissmerkmale:
Trockene harte Schneebrettlawine.
Weitere Merkmale: Flächenlawine, Oberlawine mit gemischtem Neu- und Altschneebruch, Fliesslawine, saubere trockene Ablagerung mit kantigen Schollen.
Code: A4, B8, C1, D1, E2, F2, G1, H1 oder 4811 2211.
Ort: Alp Languard, Engadin, Schweiz.

Photograph: R. Figilister, EISLF.

A. *Manner of starting*
A. *Mode de départ*
A. *Forma de iniciación*
А. *Тип начала движения*
A. *Anrissmerkmale*

Morphological classification of avalanches
Classification morphologique des avalanches
Clasificación morfológica de las avalanchas
Морфологическая классификация лавин
Morphologische Lawinenklassifikation

134

FIG. 8
Manner of starting:
Fracture of a dry surface-layer slab.
Trees immediately below the fracture are not
much affected, which suggests soft-type
slab.
Code: A3, B1 or 3100 0000.

Mode de départ:
Rupture d'une plaque superficielle sèche.
Les arbres immédiatement à l'aval de la
rupture ne sont pas trop endommagés, ce qui
suggère un type de plaque tendre.
Code: A3, B1 ou 3100 0000.

Forma de iniciación:
Fractura de placa de capa superficial seca.
Los árboles que hay inmediatamente debajo
de la fractura no se ven muy afectados, lo cual
sugiere una placa de tipo blando.
Código: A3, B1 o 3100 0000.

Тип начала движения:
Поверхность срыва сухой лавины
поверхностного слоя из снежной доски.
Деревья, расположенные ниже линии
отрыва не пострадали, что заставляет
предполагать, что это была лавина из
мягкой снежной доски.
Код: А 3, В 1   Или: 3100 0000.

Anrissmerkmale:
Anriss einer trockenen Schneebrettlawine,
Oberlawine. Bäume unmittelbar unterhalb
des Anrisses sind nicht stark in Mitleiden-
schaft gezogen, was ein weiches Schneebrett
nahelegt.
Code: A3, B1 oder 3100 0000.

Photograph: M. Shoda, Japan.

A. *Manner of starting*
A. *Mode de départ*
A. *Forma de iniciación*
А. *Тип начала движения*
A. *Anrissmerkmale*

Morphological classification of avalanches
Classification morphologique des avalanches
Clasificación morfológica de las avalanchas
Морфологическая классификация лавин
Morphologische Lawinenklassifikation

136

F<small>IG.</small> 9
Manner of starting:
Fracture of hard surface-layer slab on a
convex slope. Depth of fracture about 1 m.
Code: A4, B1, C1 or 4110 0000.

Mode de départ:
Rupture de plaque dure superficielle
sur une pente convexe.
Profondeur de la rupture 1 m environ.
Code: A4, B1, C1 ou 4110 0000.

Forma de iniciación:
Fractura de placa de capa superficial
dura en una pendiente convexa.
Espesor de la fractura aproximadamente 1 m.
Código: A4, B1, C1 o 4110 0000.

Тип начала движения:
Поверхность срыва лавины поверхностного
слоя из снежной доски, лежащей на
выпуклом склоне. Глубина положения
поверхности срыва около одного метра.
Код: А 4, В 1, С 1   Или: 4100 0000.

Anrissmerkmale:
Anriss einer harten Schneebrettlawine.
Oberlawine, an einem konvexen Hang.
Anrissmächtigkeit ca. 1 m.
Code: A4, B1, C1 oder 4110 0000.

Photograph: M. Schild, EISLF.

A. Manner of starting
A. Mode de départ
A. Forma de iniciación
A. Тип начала движения
A. Anrissmerkmale

Morphological classification of avalanches
Classification morphologique des avalanches
Clasificación morfológica de las avalanchas
Морфологическая классификация лавин
Morphologische Lawinenklassifikation

138

Fig. 10
Manner of starting:
Partial fracture of a cornice, releasing a slab
avalanche. (Possibly the slab started first
by shear fracture and portions of the cornice
fell afterwards.)
Code: A4, B3, C1, D1 or 4311 0000.

Mode de départ:
Rupture partielle d'une corniche causant
une avalanche de plaque.
(Note: il semble possible que la plaque est
partie la première par rupture au cisaillement
et que des portions de la corniche sont
tombées ultérieurement.)
Code: A4, B3, C1, D1 ou 4311 0000.

Forma de iniciación:
Fractura parcial de una cornisa que libera
una avalancha de placa (posiblemente
la placa se inició primero como consecuencia
de la fractura por cizallamiento y después
cayeron partes de la cornisa).
Código: A4, B3, C1, D1 o 4311 0000.

Тип начала движения: Отрыв части
снежного карниза вызвал лавину из снежной
доски
На переднем плане: Трещины растяжения
в снежном покрове, вызванные упавшим
снежным блоком
Код: A 4, B 3, C 1, D 1   Или: 4311 0000.

Anrissmerkmale:
Auslösung einer Schneebrettlawine durch
teilweisen Bruch einer Wächte. (Möglicher-
weise brach das Schneebrett zuerst durch
einen Scherriss los und Teile der Wächte
stürzten nachträglich ab.)
Code: A4, B3, C1, D1 oder 4311 0000.

Photograph: E. Wengi, EISLF.

139

A. Manner of starting
A. Mode de départ
A. Forma de iniciación
A. Тип начала движения
A. Anrissmerkmale

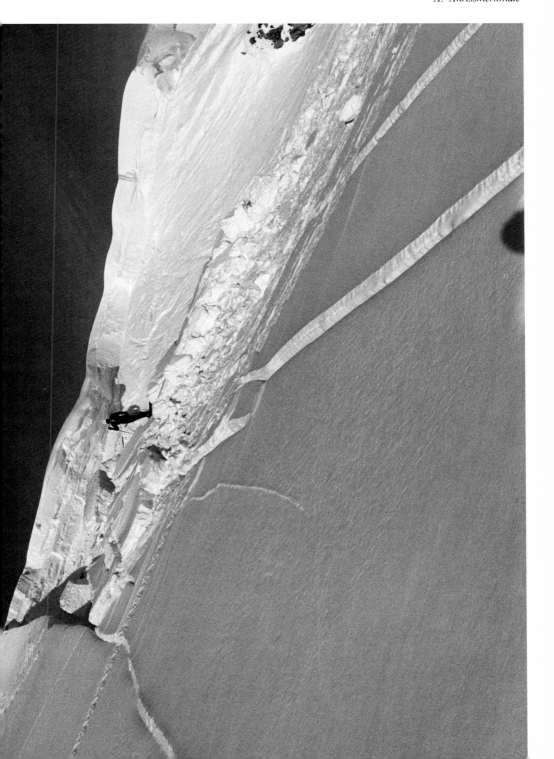

Morphological classification of avalanches
Classification morphologique des avalanches
Clasificación morfológica de las avalanchas
Морфологическая классификация лавин
Morphologische Lawinenklassifikation

FIG. 11
Manner of starting:
Detail of slab fracture.
Pliant branches of low trees (here dwarf pine, *Pinus mugo*) promote rather than prevent the formation of slab avalanches.

Mode de départ:
Détail d'une rupture de plaque.
Les branches élastiques de petits arbres (ici des pins rampants, *Pinus mugo*) favorisent plutôt qu'elles n'empêchent la formation d'avalanches de plaque.

Forma de iniciación:
Fractura de placa.
Las ramas elásticas de los árboles pequeños (en este caso pinos enanos, *Pinus mugo*) facilitan en lugar de impedir la formación de avalanchas de placa.

Тип начала движения:
Детали отрыва снежной доски:
Эластичные ветки низких деревьев (карликовая сосна, pinus mugo) больше способствуют, чем предохраняют от образовани лавин из снежных досок.

Anrissmerkmale:
Einzelheit eines Schneebrettanrisses:
Elastische Äste niedriger Bäume (hier Legföhre, *Pinus mugo*) fördern eher die Bildung von Schneebrettlawinen, als dass sie diese verhindern.

Photograph: E. Wengi, EISLF.

A. Manner of starting
A. Mode de départ
A. Forma de iniciación
A. Тип начала движения
A. Anrissmerkmale

Morphological classification of avalanches
Classification morphologique des avalanches
Clasificación morfológica de las avalanchas
Морфологическая классификация лавин
Morphologische Lawinenklassifikation

142

FIG. 12
Manner of starting
Development of slab fracture triggered by
a skier. Nearly simultaneous motion in the
coherent slab, then disintegration of the
slab into angular blocks.
Characteristics of avalanche: Dry surface-
layer slab avalanche. Probably old-snow
fracture.
Code: A2, B3, C1, D1, E2 or 2311 2000.

Mode de départ:
Développement d'une rupture de plaque
provoquée par un skieur. Presque simultanément mouvement de la plaque entière
puis désintégration de la plaque en blocs
anguleux.
Caractéristiques de l'avalanche: Avalanche
sèche superficielle. Rupture probablement
dans la vieille neige.
Code: A2, B3, C1, D1, E2 ou 2311 2000.

Forma de iniciación:
Desarrollo de fractura de placa activada
por un esquiador. Movimiento casi
simultáneo de la placa coherente y después
desintegración de la placa en bloques
angulosos.
Características de la avalancha: avalancha de
placa superficial seca, probablemente con
fractura de nieve vieja.
Código: A2, B3, C1, D1, E2 o 2311 2000.

Тип начала движения:
Развитие отрыва снежной доски, вызванное
лыжником.
Почти одновременное движение целой
доски, затем раскалывание на отдельные
угловатые блоки.
Другие характеристики: Сухая лавина
поверхностного слоя из снежной доски.
Возможно, что плоскость срыва лежит в
старом снегу.
Код: А 2, В 3, С 1, D 1, Е 2
Или: 2311, 2000.

Anrissmerkmale:
Entwicklung eines durch einen Skifahrer
ausgelösten Schneebrettanrisses. Nahezu
gleichzeitige Bewegung im zusammen-
hängenden Schneebrett, dann Zerfall des
Brettes in kantige Blöcke.
Merkmale der Lawine: Trockene Schnee-
brettlawine, Oberlawine. Vermutlich
Altschneebruch.
Code: A2, B3, C1, D1, E2 oder 2311 2000.

Photograph: R. Ludwig, Austria.

143

A. Manner of starting
A. Mode de départ
A. Forma de iniciación
A. Тип начала движения
A. Anrissmerkmale

Morphological classification of avalanches
Classification morphologique des avalanches
Clasificación morfológica de las avalanchas
Морфологическая классификация лавин
Morphologische Lawinenklassifikation

144

FIG. 13
Position of sliding surface:
Surface-layer avalanche.
Other characteristics: Dry, hard slab
avalanche.
Code: A4, B1, C1, D1 or 4111 0000.
Location: Weissfluhjoch/Davos,
Switzerland.

Position du plan de glissement:
Avalanche superficielle.
Autres caractéristiques: Avalanche de
plaque sèche, dure.
Code: A4, B1, C1, D1 ou 4111 0000.
Lieu: Weissfluhjoch/Davos, Suisse.

Posición de la superficie de deslizamiento:
Avalancha de la capa superficial.
Otras características: avalancha de placa
seca y dura.
Código: A4, B1, C1, D1 o 4111 0000.
Lugar: Weissfluhjoch/Davos, Suiza.

Положение поверхности скольжения:
Лавина поверхностного слоя.
Другие характеристики: Сухая лавина из
твердой снежной доски
Код: А 4, В 1, С 1, D 1   Или: 4111 0000.
Район: Вейсфлуйох, Давос, Швейцария

Lage der Gleitfläche:
Oberlawine.
Weitere Merkmale: Trockene, harte
Schneebrettlawine.
Code: A4, B1, C1, D1 oder 4111 0000.
Ort: Weissfluhjoch/Davos, Schweiz.

Photograph: E. Wengi, EISLF.

B. *Position of sliding surface*
B. *Position du plan de glissement*
B. *Posición de la superficie de deslizamiento*
B. *Положение поверхности скольжения*
B. *Lage der Gleitfläche*

Morphological classification of avalanches
Classification morphologique des avalanches
Clasificación morfológica de las avalanchas
Морфологическая классификация лавин
Morphologische Lawinenklassifikation

146

FIG. 14
Position of sliding surface:
Surface-layer fracture on old surface-hoar layer. A similar lower layer was not activated. (Profile excavated to expose cross-section.)
Other characteristics: Dry, hard slab avalanche.
Code: A4, B3, C1 or 4310 0000.

Position du plan de glissement:
Rupture superficielle d'une ancienne couche de givre de surface. Une couche analogue, plus bas, n'a pas été activée. (Le profil exposé montre une section verticale.)
Autres caractéristiques: Avalanche de plaque dure, sèche.
Code: A4, B3, C1 ou 4310 0000.

Posición de la superficie de deslizamiento:
Fractura superficial en una capa vieja de escarcha superficial. Una capa similar más baja no resultó activada. (El perfil ha sido excavado para dejar al descubierto la sección vertical.)
Otras características: avalancha de placa dura y seca.
Código: A4, B3, C1 o 4310 0000.

Положение поверхности скольжения.
Лавина поверхностного слоя с поверхностью срыва, лежащей на поверхности старого снежного покрова покрытой изморозью. Подобный же нижний слой не был затронут лавиной. (Вырыт шурф, чтобы показать поперечний разрез.)
Другие характеристики: Сухая лавина из твердой снежной доски.
Код: А 4, В 3, С 1 Или: 4310 0000.

Lage der Gleitfläche:
Oberlawinenbruch auf altem Oberflächenreif. Eine ähnliche, tiefere Schicht blieb inaktiv. (Anrissprofil aufgegraben.)
Weitere Merkmale: Trockene, harte Schneebrettlawine.
Code: A4, B3, C1 oder 4310 0000.

Photograph: E. Wengi, EISLF.

B. Position of sliding surface
B. Position du plan de glissement
B. Posición de la superficie de deslizamiento
B. Положение поверхности скольжения
B. Lage der Gleitfläche

Morphological classification of avalanches
Classification morphologique des avalanches
Clasificación morfológica de las avalanchas
Морфологическая классификация лавин
Morphologische Lawinenklassifikation

148

FIG. 15
Position of sliding surface:
Full depth avalanche (fracture of depth hoar layer).
Other characteristics: Hard slab fracture on convex slope. Dry, unconfined flow avalanche with clean, dry deposition in angular blocks.
Code: A4, B4, C1, D1, E2, F2, G1, H1 or 4411 2211.

Position du plan de glissement:
Avalanche de fond (rupture d'une couche de givre de profondeur).
Autres caractéristiques: Rupture de plaque dure sur une pente convexe. Avalanche de versant coulante, sèche, avec dépôt propre et sec en blocs anguleux.
Code: A4, B4, C1, D1, E2, F2, G1, H1 ou 4411 2211.

Posición de la superficie de deslizamiento:
Avalancha en profundidad (fractura de una capa de escarcha profunda).
Otras características: fractura de placa dura en pendiente convexa. Avalancha seca de flujo sin confinar, con depósito limpio y seco en bloques angulosos.
Código: A4, B4, C1, D1, E2, F2, G1, H1 o 4411 2211.

Положение поверхности скольжения:
Лавина полной глубины (поверхность срыва по слою глубинной изморози).
Другие характеристики: Лавина из твердой снежной доски на выпуклом склоне. Сухая, неканализованная текучая лавина с чистым сухим снегом, состоящим из угловатых блоков в зоне отложения.
Код: A 4, B 4, C 1, D 1, E 2, F 2, G 1, H 1
Или: 4411, 225

Lage der Gleitfläche:
Bodenlawine (Bruch einer Schwimm-schneelage).
Weitere Merkmale: Harter Schneebrett-anriss an konvexem Hang. Trockene Flächenlawine. Fliesslawine mit reiner, trockener Ablagerung in kantigen Blöcken.
Code: A4, B4, C1, D1, E2, F2, G1, H1 oder 4411 2211.

Photograph: E. Bucher, EISLF.

B. Position of sliding surface
B. Position du plan de glissement
B. Posición de la superficie de deslizamiento
B. Положение поверхности скольжения
B. Lage der Gleitfläche

Morphological classification of avalanches
Classification morphologique des avalanches
Clasificación morfológica de las avalanchas
Морфологическая классификация лавин
Morphologische Lawinenklassifikation

150

FIG. 16
Position of sliding surface:
Full-depth avalanche (failure in depth hoar layer).
Other characteristics: Hard-dry-slab avalanche (artificial release).
Code: A4, B4, C1, J4 or 4410 0000 4.
Location: Alta, Utah, United States.

Position du plan de glissement:
Avalanche de fond (rupture d'une couche de givre de profondeur).
Autres caractéristiques: Avalanche de plaque sèche et dure (déclenchement artificiel).
Code: A4, B4, C1, J4 ou 4410 0000 4.
Lieu: Alta, Utah, Etats-Unis d'Amérique.

Posición de la superficie de deslizamiento:
Fractura profunda (en una capa de escarcha profunda).
Otras características: avalancha de placa seca y dura (iniciación artificial).
Código: A4, B4, C1, J4 o 4410 0000 4.
Lugar: Alta, Utah, Estados Unidos.

Положение поверхности скольжения:
Лавина полной глубины (срыв в слое глубинной изморози).
Другие характеристики:
Сухая лавина из твердой снежной доски (искусственный сброс).
Код: A 4, B 4, C 1, J 4   Или: 4410 0000 4.
Район: Альта, Юта, США

Lage der Gleitfläche:
Bodenlawine (Bruch auf Schwimm-schneelage).
Weitere Merkmale: Harte, trockene Schneebrettlawine (künstl. Auslösung).
Code: A4, B4, C1, J4 oder 4410 0000 4.
Ort: Alta, Utah, U.S.A.

Photograph: E. R. LaChapelle, United States.

B. Position of sliding surface
B. Position du plan de glissement
B. Posición de la superficie de deslizamiento
B. Положение поверхности скольжения
B. Lage der Gleitfläche

Morphological classification of avalanches
Classification morphologique des avalanches
Clasificación morfológica de las avalanchas
Морфологическая классификация лавин
Morphologische Lawinenklassifikation

152

FIG. 17
Position of sliding surface:
Full-depth avalanche (despite snow veil remaining on the ground).
Other characteristics: Dry-slab, unconfined flow-avalanche. Dry, clean, coarse deposit.
Code: A2, B4, C1, D1, E2, F1, G1, H1 or 2411 2111.

Position du plan de glissement:
Avalanche de fond (en dépit du voile de neige restant sur le sol).
Autres caractéristiques: Avalanche de plaque sèche. Avalanche coulante de versant. Dépôt sec, propre, grossier.
Code: A2, B4, C1, D1, E2, F1, G1, H1 ou 2411 2111.

Posición de la superficie de deslizamiento:
Avalancha en profundidad (a pesar del velo de nieve que queda sobre el terreno).
Otras características: avalancha de placa seca. Avalancha de flujo sin confinar. Depósito grueso, limpio y seco.
Código: A2, B4, C1, D1, E2, F1, G1, H1 o 2411 2111.

Положение поверхности скольжения:
Лавина полной глубины (несмотря на то, что снежная пелена покрывает землю).
Другие характеристики: Сухая неканализованная лавина из снежной доски с сухим, чистым крупнокомковатым снегом в зоне отложения.
Код: А 2, В 4, С 1, D 1, Е 2, F 1, G 1, Н 1
Или: 2411, 2111

Lage der Gleitfläche:
Bodenlawine (trotz auf dem Boden verbleibendem Schneeschleier).
Weitere Merkmale: Trockene Schneebrettlawine. Flächenlawine, Fliesslawine. Trockene, reine, grobe Ablagerung.
Code: A2, B4, C1, D1, E2, F1, G1, H1 oder 2411 2111.

Photograph: R. Figilister, EISLF.

B. Position of sliding surface
B. Position du plan de glissement
B. Posición de la superficie de deslizamiento
B. Положение поверхности скольжения
B. Lage der Gleitfläche

Morphological classification of avalanches
Classification morphologique des avalanches
Clasificación morfológica de las avalanchas
Морфологическая классификация лавин
Morphologische Lawinenklassifikation

154

FIG. 18
Position of sliding surface:
Full-depth avalanche.
Other characteristics: Unconfined wet-slab
flow-avalanche (note melt channels in
undisturbed snow). The avalanche started
after a glide crack had opened.
Code: A2, B4, C2, D1, E2 or 2421 2000.

Положение поверхности скольжения:
Лавина полной глубины.
Другие характеристики: Мокрая лавина из
снежной доски (видны каналы стока воды
в ненарушенном снежном покрове).
Неканализованная текучая лавина.
Лавина зародилась после раскрытия
трещины, образовавшейся в результате
сползания снега.
Код: А 2, В 4, С 2, D 1, Е 2   Или: 2421 2000

Position du plan de glissement:
Avalanche de fond.
Autres caractéristiques: Avalanche de
plaque humide (notez les rigoles de fusion
dans la neige en place). Avalanche coulante
de versant. L'avalanche est partie après
la formation d'une crevasse due à la
reptation.
Code: A2, B4, C2, D1, E2 ou 2421 2000.

Lage der Gleitfläche:
Bodenlawine.
Weitere Merkmale: Nasse Schneebrett-
lawine (beachte Schmelzrinnen in
ungestörtem Schnee). Flächenlawine,
Fliesslawine. Die Lawine ging nieder,
nachdem sich eine Gleitspalte geöffnet hatte.
Code: A2, B4, C2, D1, E2 oder 2421 2000.

Posición de la superficie de deslizamiento:
Avalancha en profundidad.
Otras características: avalancha de placa
húmeda (obsérvense los canales de
fusión en la nieve intacta). Avalancha de flujo
sin confinar. La avalancha se inició después
de que se abriese una grieta de deslizamiento.
Código: A2, B4, C2, D1, E2 o 2421 2000.

Photograph: M. Shoda, Japan.

B. Position of sliding surface
B. Position du plan de glissement
B. Posición de la superficie de deslizamiento
B. Положение поверхности скольжения
B. Lage der Gleitfläche

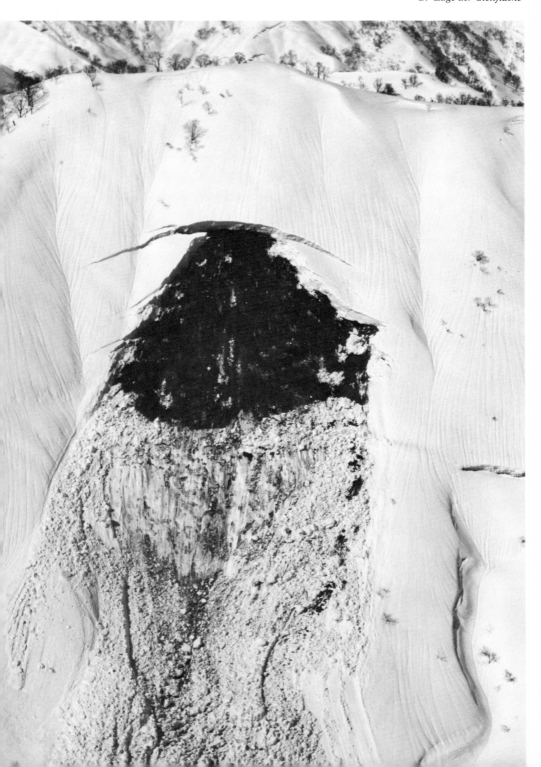

Morphological classification of avalanches
Classification morphologique des avalanches
Clasificación morfológica de las avalanchas
Морфологическая классификация лавин
Morphologische Lawinenklassifikation

156

FIG. 19
Position of sliding surface:
Mixed surface-layer and full-depth (on the left) fracture in old snow.
Other characteristics: Dry, hard, unconfined slab avalanche. Dry clean deposit in angular blocks.
Code: A4, B7, C1, D1, E2, F3, G1, H1 or 4711 2311.
Location: Weissfluhjoch/Davos, Switzerland.

Position du plan de glissement:
Avalanche superficielle et de fond (à gauche) dans la vieille neige.
Autres caractéristiques: Avalanche de versant de plaque sèche et dure. Dépôt sec et propre en blocs anguleux.
Code: A4, B7, C1, D1, E2, F3, G1, H1 ou 4711 2311.
Lieu: Weissfluhjoch/Davos, Suisse.

Posición de la superficie de deslizamiento:
Fractura superficial y de profundidad (lado izquierdo) y nieve vieja mezclada.
Otras características: avalancha de placa seca, dura y sin confinar: depósito limpio y seco en bloques angulosos.
Código: A4, B7, C1, D1, E2, F3, G1, H1 o 4711 2311.
Lugar: Weissfluhjoch/Davos, Suiza.

Положение поверхности скольжения:
Смешанная лавина поверхностного слоя и полной глубины (левая сторона фотографии) поверхностью срыва в старом снежном покрове.
Другие характеристики: Сухая, неканализованная лавина из твердой снежной доски. Сухие чистые отложения, состоящие из угловатых блоков.
Код: А 4, В 7, С 1, D 1, Е 2, F 3, G 1, Н 1 Или: 4711 2311.
Вейсфлуйох, Давос, Швейцария

Lage der Gleitfläche:
Gemischte Oberlawine mit Altschneebruch und Bodenlawine (links auf Bild).
Weitere Merkmale: Trockene, harte Schneebrettlawine, Flächenlawine. Trockene, reine Ablagerung mit kantigen Blöcken.
Code: A4, B7, C1, D1, E2, F3, G1, H1 oder 4711 2311.
Ort: Weissfluhjoch/Davos, Schweiz.

Photograph: E. Wengi, EISLF.

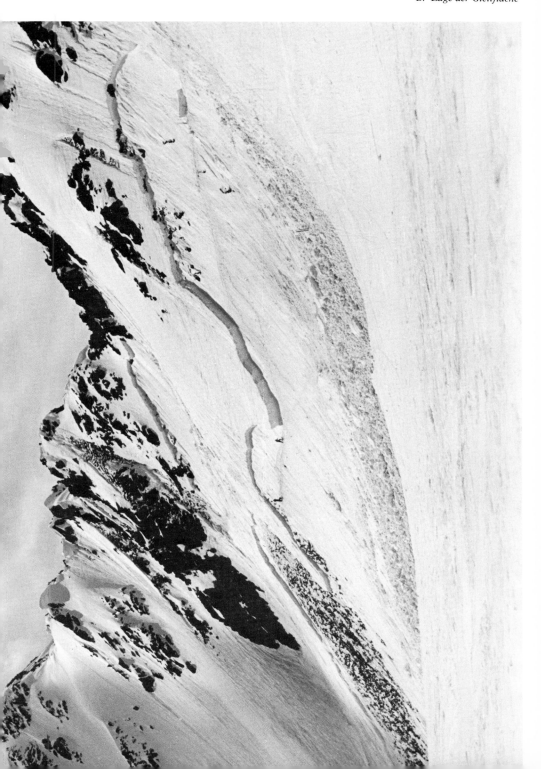

157

B. *Position of sliding surface*
B. *Position du plan de glissement*
B. *Posición de la superficie de deslizamiento*
В. *Положение поверхности скольжения*
B. *Lage der Gleitfläche*

Morphological classification of avalanches
Classification morphologique des avalanches
Clasificación morfológica de las avalanchas
Морфологическая классификация лавин
Morphologische Lawinenklassifikation

158

FIG. 20
Position of sliding surface:
Full depth slab avalanche with extensive
propagation of tensile fracture. Parts of the
slab stayed in place after fracture due to
activated friction.
Code: A2, B4, D1 or 2401.
Location: Gornergrat, Zermatt, Switzerland.

Position du plan de glissement:
Avalanche de fond en plaque, avec grande
extension d'une fracture de tension.
Des fragments de la plaque sont restés
en place après la rupture en raison du
frottement actif.
Code: A2, B4, D1 ou 2401 0000.
Lieu: Gornergrat, Zermatt, Suisse.

Posición de la superficie de deslizamiento:
Avalancha de placa en profundidad con una
extensa propagación de fractura por tracción.
Algunos fragmentos de la placa se mantu-
vieron en posición después de la fractura
debida a fricción activada.
Código: A2, B4, D1 o 2401.
Lugar: Gornergrat, Zermatt, Suiza.

Положение поверхности скольжения:
Лавина полной глубины из снежной доски
с широким распространением трещин
растяжения. Часть снежной доски осталась
на месте из-за сильного трения.
Код: А 2, В 4, D 1   Или: 2401
Район: Горнерграт, Церматт, Швейцария

Lage der Gleitfläche:
Bodenlawine.
Schneebrettlawine mit weitreichender Fort-
pflanzung des Zugrisses. Teile des Schnee-
brettes blieben nach dem Bruch wegen der
aktivierten Bodenreibung haften.
Code: A2, B4, D1 oder 2401.
Ort: Gornergrat, Zermatt, Schweiz.

Photograph: A. Roch, EISLF.

B. *Position of sliding surface*
B. *Position du plan de glissement*
B. *Posición de la superficie de deslizamiento*
B. *Положение поверхности скольжения*
B. *Lage der Gleitfläche*

FIG. 21

Liquid water in snow:
Absent (dry-snow avalanche).
Nearly simultaneous loose-snow and slab avalanches. Time sequence, left to right.
Left-hand side: Three dry loose-snow avalanches with new snow fractures.
Other characteristics: Unconfined flow avalanches with fine dry clean deposit.
Code: A1, B2, C1, D1, E2, F4, G1, H1 or 1211 2411.
Right-hand side: Two dry soft-slab avalanches with partly new snow, partly old-snow fracture.
Other characteristics: Unconfined flow avalanches with fine (left) and coarse (right) clean deposits.
Code: A3, B8, C1, D1, E2, F1, G1, H1 or 3811 2111.
Location: Weissfluhjoch/Davos.

Eau liquide dans la neige:
Absente (avalanche de neige sèche).
Avalanches presque simultanées de neige sans cohésion et de plaque. Départs se succédant de gauche à droite.
Côté gauche: 3 avalanches de neige sèche sans cohésion avec rupture dans la neige fraîche.
Autres caractéristiques: Avalanches de versant coulantes avec dépôts fins, secs et propres.
Code: A1, B2, C1, D1, E2, F4, G1, H1 ou 1211 2411.
Côté droit: 2 avalanches de plaque tendre avec rupture partiellement dans la neige fraîche, partiellement dans la vieille neige.
Autres caractéristiques: Avalanches coulantes de versant avec dépôts propres, fins (à gauche) et grossiers (à droite).
Code: A3, B8, C1, D1, E2, F1, G1, H1 ou 3811 2111.
Lieu: Weissfluhjoch/Davos, Suisse.

Agua líquida en la nieve:
Ausente (avalancha de nieve seca).
Avalanchas de placa y de nieve suelta casi simultáneas. Secuencia en el tiempo de izquierda a derecha.
Lado izquierdo: tres avalanchas de nieve suelta seca con fracturas de nieve nueva.
Otras características: avalanchas de flujo sin confinar con depósito limpio, seco y fino.
Código: A1, B2, C1, D1, E2, F4, G1, H1 o 1211 2411.

Lado derecho: dos avalanchas de placa blanda y seca, con fracturas parcialmente de nieve vieja y parcialmente de nieve nueva.
Otras características: avalanchas de flujo sin confinar con depósitos limpios, finos (izquierda) y gruesos (derecha).
Código: A3, B8, C1, D1, E2, F1, G1, H1 o 3811 2111.
Lugar: Weissfluhjoch/Davos, Suiza.

Жидкая вода в снегу:
Отсутствует (сухая лавина).
Почти одновременные лавины из рыхлого снега и снежных досок. Последовательность их зарождения по времени, слева направо.
Левая сторона: 3 сухие лавины из рыхлого снега с новерхностью срыва в новом снеге.
Другие характеристики: Неканализованные текучие лавины с мелкокомковатым (слева) и крупнокомковатнм (справа) чистым снегом в зоне отложнеия
Код: А 1, В 2, С 1, D 1, E 2, F 4, G 1, H 1 Или: 1211, 2411
Правая сторона: Две сухие лавины из мягкой снежной доски с поверхностью срыва, лежащей частично в старом снегу, частично в новом снегу.

Flüssiges Wasser im Schnee:
Fehlend (trocken). Trockenschneelawine.
Nahezu gleichzeitig entstandene Lockerschnee- und Schneebrettlawinen. Zeitfolge von links nach rechts.
Links Seite: 3 trockene Lockerschneelawinen mit Neuschneeebruch.
Weitere Merkmale: Flächenlawinen mit feiner, trockener, reiner Ablagerung.
Code: A1, B2, C1, D1, E2, F4, G1, H1 oder 1211 2411.
Rechte Seite: 2 trockene, weiche Schneebrettlawinen mit teilweise Neuschnee- teilweise Altschneebruch.
Weitere Merkmale: Flächenlawinen, Fliesslawinen mit feiner (links) und grober (rechts) reiner Ablagerung.
Code: A3, B8, C1, D1, E2, F1, G1, H1 oder 3811 2111.
Ort: Weissfluhjoch/Davos, Schweiz.

Photograph: E. Wengi, EISLF.

C. Liquid water in snow
C. Eau liquide dans la neige
C. Agua líquida en la nieve
C. Жидкая вода в снегу
C. Flüssiges Wasser im Schnee

Morphological classification of avalanches
Classification morphologique des avalanches
Clasificación morfológica de las avalanchas
Морфологическая классификация лавин
Morphologische Lawinenklassifikation

162

FIG. 22
Liquid water in snow:
Present (wet-snow avalanche).
Wet full-depth loose-snow avalanche.
Other characteristics: Unconfined flow
avalanche with clean, coarse, wet deposit.
Code: A1, B4, C2, D1, E2, F3, G2, H1
or 1421 2321.
Location: Dorfberg, Davos, Switzerland.

Eau liquide dans la neige:
Présente (avalanche de neige mouillée).
Avalanche de fond de neige sans cohésion.
Autres caractéristiques: Avalanche coulante,
de versant, avec dépôt propre, grossier,
humide.
Code: A1, B4, C2, D1, E2, F3, G2, H1
ou 1421 2321.
Lieu: Dorfberg, Davos, Suisse.

Agua líquida en la nieve:
Presente (avalancha de nieve húmeda).
Avalancha profunda de nieve suelta.
Otras características: avalancha de flujo sin
confinar, con depósito limpio, grueso
y húmedo.
Código: A1, B4, C2, D1, E2, F3, G2, H1
o 1421 2321.
Lugar: Dorfberg, Davos, Suiza.

Жидкая вода в снегу:
Имеется (мокрая лавина).
Мокрая лавина полной глубины из
рыхлого снега.
Другие характеристики: Неканализованная
текучая лавина с чистыми, крупнокомко-
ватыми мокрыми отложениями.
Код: А 1, В 4, С 2, D 1, Е 2, F 3, G 2, H 1
Или: 1421 2321.
Район: Дорфберг, Давос, Швейцария

Flüssiges Wasser im Schnee:
Vorhanden (nass). Nassschneelawine.
Nasse Lockerschneelawine. Bodenlawine.
Weitere Merkmale: Flächenlawine. Fliess-
lawine mit reiner, grober Ablagerung.
Code: A1, B4, C2, D1, E2, F3, G2, H1
oder 1421 2321.
Ort: Dorfberg, Davos, Schweiz.

Photograph: E. Wengi, EISLF.

C. Liquid water in snow
C. Eau liquide dans la neige
C. Agua líquida en la nieve
С. Жидкая вода в снегу
C. Flüssiges Wasser im Schnee

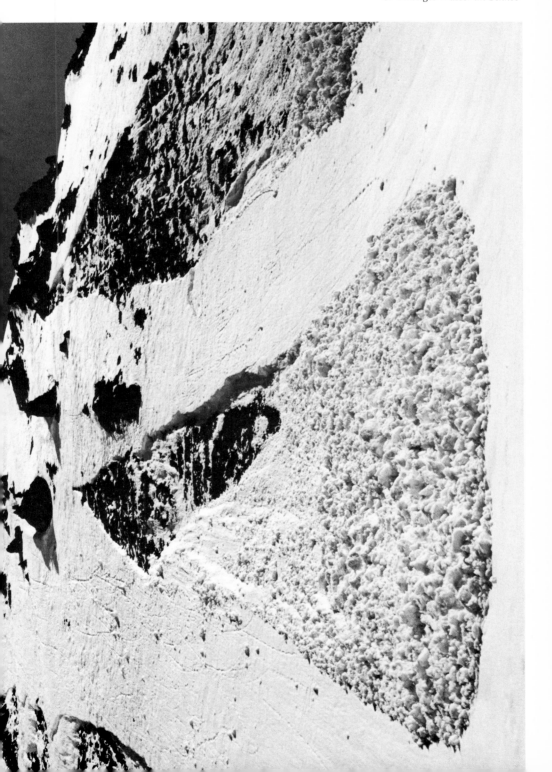

Morphological classification of avalanches
Classification morphologique des avalanches
Clasificación morfológica de las avalanchas
Морфологическая классификация лавин
Morphologische Lawinenklassifikation

164

FIG. 23

Form of path:
Unconfined avalanche on open, smooth
terrain without particular relief characteristics. Homogeneous slope up to the crest.
Other characteristics: Dry-slab avalanche
with single loose-snow fractures (cornice
apparently not involved). Surface-layer
flow avalanche with (probably) powder
component. Clean, dry, predominantly
fine deposit.
Code: A2, B1, C1, D1, E2, F4, G1, H1
or 2111 2411.
Location: Gaudergrat, Parsenn, Switzerland.

Tracé du parcours:
Avalanche de versant sur un terrain ouvert,
lisse, sans caractère particulier du relief.
Pente homogène jusqu'à la crête.
Autres caractéristiques: Avalanche de
plaque sèche avec ruptures isolées en
neige sans cohésion (corniche apparemment
non concernée par l'avalanche). Avalanche
superficielle, coulante avec (probablement)
une composante poudreuse. Dépôt propre,
sec, à dominance fine.
Code: A2, B1, C1, D1, E2, F4, G1, H1
ou 2111 2411.
Lieu: Gaudergrat, Parsenn, Suisse.

Forma de la senda:
Avalancha sin confinar en terreno abierto y
liso, sin particulares características de relieve.
Pendiente homogénea hasta la cresta.
Otras características: avalancha de placa seca
con fracturas simples de nieve suelta
(al parecer la cornisa no se vio involucrada).
Avalancha de capa superficial y de flujo, con
componente en polvo (probablemente).
Depósito limpio, seco y dominante fino.
Código: A2, B1, C1, D1, E2, F4, G1, H1
o 2111 2411.
Lugar: Gaudergrat, Parsenn, Suiza.

Форма пути:
Неканализованная лавина на ровном,
гладком склоне без специфического
рельефа. Однородный склон до гребня.
Другие характеристики: Сухая лавина
из снежной доски с единственной линией
отрыва в рыхлом снегу (карниз, очевидно,
не вовлечен в движение). Лавина поверхностного слоя. Текучая лавина с (возможно)
пылевой компонентой.
Чистые, сухие, преимущественно мелкокомковатые отложения.
Код: А 2, В 1, С 1, D 1, Е 2, F 4, G 1, H 1
Или: 2111, 2411
Район: Гаудерграт, Парценн, Швейцария

Form der Sturzbahn:
Flächenlawine auf offenem, ebenmässigem
Gelände ohne besonderes Relief. Gleich-
mässige Neigung bis hinauf zum Bergkamm.
Weitere Merkmale: Trockene Schneebrett-
lawine mit einzelnen Lockerschneeanrissen.
Fliesslawine mit (wahrscheinlich) Staub-
anteil. Reine, trockene, vorwiegend feine
Ablagerung.
Code: A2, B1, C1, D1, E2, F4, G1, H1
oder 2111 2411.
Ort: Gaudergrat, Parsenn, Schweiz.

Photograph: E. Bucher, EISLF.

Morphological classification of avalanches
Classification morphologique des avalanches
Clasificación morfológica de las avalanchas
Морфологическая классификация лавин
Morphologische Lawinenklassifikation

166

FIG. 24
Form of path:
Channelled avalanche.
Other characteristics: Flow avalanche with
mixed dry and wet, coarse and partly
contaminated deposit.
Code: D2, E2, F1, G7, H7 or 0002 2177.
Location: Wilerlaui, Erstfeld, Switzerland.

Tracé du parcours:
Avalanche de couloir.
Autres caractéristiques: Avalanche coulante
avec dépôt mixte sec et humide, grossier
et partiellement souillé.
Code: D2, E2, F1, G7, H7 ou 0002 2177.
Lieu: Wilerlaui, Erstfeld, Suisse.

Forma de la senda:
Avalancha acanalada.
Otras características: avalancha de flujo con
depósito mezclado seco y húmedo,
grueso y parcialmente contaminado.
Código: D2, E2, F1, G7, H7 o 0002 2177.
Lugar: Wilerlaui, Erstfeld, Suiza.

Форма пути:
Канализованная лавина.
Другие характеристики: Текучая лавина
из смеси сухого и мокрого снега,
мелкокомковатые и частично загрязненные
отложения.
Код: D 2, E 2, F 1, C 7, H 7
Или: 0002, 2177.
Район: Вилерлауи, Эрстфилд, Швейцария

Form der Sturzbahn:
Runsenlawine.
Weitere Merkmale: Fliesslawine mit
gemischt trockener und nasser, grober und
teilweise unreiner Ablagerung.
Code: D2, E2, F1, G7, H7 oder 0002 2177.
Ort: Wilerlaui, Erstfeld, Schweiz.

Photograph: E. Saxer, Switzerland.

D. Form of path
D. Tracé du parcours
D. Forma de la senda
D. Форма пути
D. Form der Sturzbahn

Morphological classification of avalanches
Classification morphologique des avalanches
Clasificación morfológica de las avalanchas
Морфологическая классификация лавин
Morphologische Lawinenklassifikation

168

FIG. 25
Form of path:
Channelled avalanche through forest area.
Channel not pronounced.
Code: D2 or 0002 0000.
Location: Berthoud Falls, Colorado,
United States.

Tracé du parcours:
Avalanche de couloir à travers une zone de
forêt. Couloir peu prononcé.
Code: D2 ou 0002 0000.
Lieu: Berthoud Falls, Colorado,
Etats-Unis d'Amérique.

Forma de la senda:
Avalancha acanalada a través de una zona de
bosque. Canal poco pronunciado.
Código: D2 o 0002 0000.
Lugar: Berthoud Falls, Colorado,
Estados Unidos.

Форма пути:
Канализованная лавина на залесенном
склоне. Лавинный лоток выражен слабо.
Код: 02   Или: 0002 0000.
Район: Бертхауд-Фоллс, Колорадо, США.

Form der Sturzbahn:
Runsenlawine durch Waldzone. Runse
nicht ausgeprägt.
Code: D2 oder 0002 0000.
Ort: Berthoud Falls, Colorado, U.S.A.

Photograph: H. Frutiger, EISLF.

D. *Form of path*
D. *Tracé du parcours*
D. *Forma de la senda*
D. *Форма пути*
D. *Form der Sturzbahn*

Morphological classification of avalanches
Classification morphologique des avalanches
Clasificación morfológica de las avalanchas
Морфологическая классификация лавин
Morphologische Lawinenklassifikation

170

FIG. 26
Form of path:
Mixed unconfined and channelled avalanche.
Unconfined starting zone leading into a
number of separate channels.
Other characteristics: Slab avalanche with
surface-layer fracture.
Code: A2, B1, D7 or 2107 0000.

Tracé du parcours:
Avalanche mixte de versant et de couloir.
Zone de départ sur versant alimentant
plusieurs couloirs séparés.
Autres caractéristiques: Avalanche de
plaque avec rupture superficielle.
Code: A2, B1, D7 ou 2107 0000.

Forma de la senda:
Avalancha mixta, acanalada y sin confinar.
Zona de inicio sin confinar alimentando
varios canales separados.
Otras características: avalancha de placa con
fractura de la capa superficial.
Código: A2, B1, D7 o 2107 0000.

Форма пути:
Смешанная неканализованная и канализованная лавина. Неканализованная зона
зарождения переходит в несколько
отдельных лотков.
Другиа характеристики: Лавина поверхностного слоя из снежных досок.
Код: A 2, B 1, D 7   Или: 2107, 0000.

Form der Sturzbahn:
Gemischte Flächen- und Runsenlawine.
Ein flächiges Anrissgebiet mündet in eine
Anzahl von getrennten Runsen.
Weitere Merkmale: Schneebrettlawine.
Oberlawine.
Code: A2, B1, D7 oder 2107 0000.

Photograph: M. Shoda, Japan.

D. Form of path
D. Tracé du parcours
D. Forma de la senda
D. Форма пути
D. Form der Sturzbahn

Morphological classification of avalanches
Classification morphologique des avalanches
Clasificación morfológica de las avalanchas
Морфологическая классификация лавин
Morphologische Lawinenklassifikation

172

FIG. 27
Form of movement:
Powder avalanche. Full powder development due to cascade formation.
Other characteristics: Dry confined avalanche.
Code: C1, D2, E1 or 0012 1000.
Location: Daubenhorn, Leukerbad, Switzerland.

Type de mouvement:
Avalanche de poudreuse. Grand développement de la poudreuse en raison de la formation en cascade.
Autres caractéristiques: Avalanche de couloir sèche.
Code: C1, D2, E1 ou 0012 1000.
Lieu: Daubenhorn, Leukerbad, Suisse.

Forma de movimiento:
Avalancha de polvo. Desarrollo completo de polvo debido a la formación de cascada.
Otras características: avalancha acanalada seca.
Código: C1, D2, E1 o 0012 1000.
Lugar: Daubenhorn, Leukerbad, Suiza.

Тип движения:
Пылевая лавина. Развитие полностью пылевой лавины обусловлено серией ступеней.
Другие характеристики: Канализованная лавина из сухого снега.
Код: C 1, D 2, E 1 Или 0012 1000
Район: Даубенхорн, Лейк, Швейцария

Form der Bewegung:
Staublawine. Völlige Staubentwicklung wegen der Kaskadenbildung.
Weitere Merkmale: Trockene Runsenlawine.
Code: C1, D2, E1 oder 0012 1000.
Ort: Daubenhorn, Leukerbad, Schweiz.

Photograph: Engelberger, Switzerland.

E. Form of movement
E. Type de mouvement
E. Forma de movimiento
E. Тип движения
E. Form der Bewegung

Morphological classification of avalanches
Classification morphologique des avalanches
Clasificación morfológica de las avalanchas
Морфологическая классификация лавин
Morphologische Lawinenklassifikation

174

FIG. 28
Form of movement:
Powder avalanche (dominant powder
component).
Other characteristics: Dry unconfined
avalanche (artificially triggered).
Code: C1, D1, E1, J4 or 0011 1000 4.
Location: Lavin, Engadine, Switzerland.

Type de mouvement:
Avalanche de poudreuse (composante
poudreuse dominante).
Autres caractéristiques: Avalanche sèche de
versant (déclenchée artificiellement).
Code: C1, D1, E1, J4 ou 0011 1000 4.
Lieu: Lavin, Engadine, Suisse.

Forma de movimiento:
Avalancha de polvo (componente predo-
minante polvo).
Otras características: avalancha seca sin
confinar (activada artificialmente).
Código: C1, D1, E1, J4 o 0011 1000 4.
Lugar: Lavin, Engadine, Suiza.

Тип движения:
Пылевая лавина (преобладает пылевая
компонента)
Другие характеристики: Неканализованная
лавина из сухого снега (искусственный
спуск)
Район: Лавин, Энгадин, Швейцария

Form der Bewegung:
Staublawine (vorherrschender Staubanteil).
Weitere Merkmale: Trockene Flächen-
lawine (künstlich ausgelöst).
Code: C1, D1, E1, J4 oder 0011 1000 4.
Ort: Lavin, Engadin, Schweiz.

Photograph: W. Porton, Switzerland.

E. Form of movement
E. Type de mouvement
E. Forma de movimiento
E. Тип движения
E. Form der Bewegung

Morphological classification of avalanches
Classification morphologique des avalanches
Clasificación morfológica de las avalanchas
Морфологическая классификация лавин
Morphologische Lawinenklassifikation

FIG. 29
Form of movement:
Mixed flow and powder avalanche. At this stage a predominant flow avalanche with increasing powder component (artificially triggered).
Other characteristics: Dry, soft-slab, surface-layer avalanche with mixed new and old snow fracture (nearly full depth), unconfined path.
Code: A3, B8, C1, D1, E7, J4 or 3811 7000 4.
Location: Hauptertäli, Langwies, Switzerland.

Type de mouvement:
Avalanche mixte poudreuse et coulante.
A ce stade, coulante dominante avec composante poudreuse croissante (déclenchée artificiellement).
Autres caractéristiques: Avalanche superficielle de plaque tendre et sèche avec rupture mixte en neige fraîche et vieille neige (presque une avalanche de fond); avalanche de versant.
Code: A3, B8, C1, D1, E7, J4 ou 3811 7000 4.
Lieu: Hauptertäli, Langwies, Suisse.

Forma de movimiento:
Avalancha en polvo y de flujo mixto. En esta fase, avalancha de flujo dominante con componente creciente de polvo (iniciado artificialmente).
Otras características: avalancha de placa blanda y seca. Avalancha de capa superficial con fractura de nieve nueva y vieja mezcladas (cerca de la profundidad máxima), senda sin confinar.
Código: A3, B8, C1, D1, E7, J4 o 3811 7000 4.
Lugar: Hauptertäli, Langwies, Suiza.

Тип движения:
Смешанная текучая и пылевая лавина. На данной стадии преобладает текучая составляющая с увеличивающейся пылевой компонентой (искусственный спуск).
Другие характеристики: Лавина из сухих мягких досок. Неканализованная лавина поверхностного слоя с поверхностью срыва как в новом так и в старом снежном покрове (почти полной глубины).
Код: A 3, B 8, C 1, D 1, E 7, 4
Или: 3811, 7000, 4
Район: Хауптертели, Лангвис, Швейцария

Form der Bewegung:
Gemischte Fliess- und Staublawine. In diesem Stadium vorherrschende Fliesslawine mit zunehmendem Staubanteil (künstlich ausgelöst).
Weitere Merkmale: Trockene, weiche Schneebrettlawine, Oberlawine mit gemischtem Neu- und Altschneebruch (nahezu Bodenlawine). Flächenlawine.
Code: A3, B8, C1, D1, E7, J4 oder 3811 7000 4.
Ort: Hauptertäli, Langwies, Schweiz.

Photograph: J. Neher, EISLF.

E. Form of movement
E. Type de mouvement
E. Forma de movimiento
E. Тип движения
E. Form der Bewegung

Morphological classification of avalanches
Classification morphologique des avalanches
Clasificación morfológica de las avalanchas
Морфологическая классификация лавин
Morphologische Lawinenklassifikation

178

FIG. 30
Form of movement:
Powder avalanche: bulk of snow dissipated
as snow cloud. Low-density cloud stays
behind frontal zone of higher density.
Other characteristics: Unconfined dry-snow
avalanche.
Code: C1, D1, E1 or 0011 1000.
Location: Col du Lautaret, France.

Type de mouvement:
Avalanche de poudreuse. La plupart de la
masse de neige est dissipée en nuage.
Le nuage de densité faible reste derrière
la zone frontale de densité élevée.
Autres caractéristiques: Avalanche de
versant sèche.
Code: C1, D1, E1 ou 0011 1000.
Lieu: Col du Lautaret, France.

Forma de movimiento:
Avalancha de polvo. La mayor parte de la
nieve se dispersa en forma de nube. La nube
de baja densidad queda detrás de la zona
frontal de mayor densidad.
Otras características: avalancha sin confinar
de nieve seca.
Código: C1, D1, E1 o 0011 1000.
Lugar: Col du Lautaret, Francia.

Тип движения:
Пылевая лавина. Основная масса снега
распространяется в виде снежного облака.
Часть облака с более низкой плотностью
остается сзади фронтальной более плотной
зоны.
Другие характеристики: Неканализованная
лавина из сухого снега.
Код: C 1, D 1, E 1   Или: 0011, 1000
Район: Кол-дю-Лотаре, Франция

Form der Bewegung:
Staublawine. Hauptmasse des Schnees als
Schneewolke aufgewirbelt. Die Wolke von
niederer Dichte bleibt hinter der frontalen
Zone von höherer Dichte zurück.
Weitere Merkmale: Trockene Flächen-
lawine.
Code: C1, D1, E1 oder 0011 1000.
Ort: Col du Lautaret, Frankreich.

Photograph: L. Rey, France.

E. *Form of movement*
E. *Type de mouvement*
E. *Forma de movimiento*
Е. *Тип движения*
E. *Form der Bewegung*

Morphological classification of avalanches
Classification morphologique des avalanches
Clasificación morfológica de las avalanchas
Морфологическая классификация лавин
Morphologische Lawinenklassifikation

FIG. 31
Form of movement:
Combined flow and powder avalanche.
Progressive disintegration of snow blocks.
Other characteristics: Dry-snow avalanche.
Code: C1, E7 or 0010 7000.
Location: Col du Lautaret, France.

Type de mouvement:
Avalanche mixte poudreuse et coulante.
Désagrégation progressive de blocs de
neige.
Autres caractéristiques: Avalanche de
neige sèche.
Code: C1, E7 ou 0010 7000.
Lieu: Col du Lautaret, France.

Forma de movimiento:
Avalancha combinada de flujo y polvo.
Disgregación progresiva de bloques de nieve.
Otras características: avalancha de nieve seca.
Código: C1, E7 o 0010 7000.
Lugar: Col du Lautaret, Francia.

Тип движения:
Комбинированная текучая и пылевая
лавина с прогрессирующим разрушением
снежных блоков.
Другие характеристики: Сухая лавина.
Код: E 7 Или: 0010, 7000
Район: Кол-дю-Лотаре, Франция

Form der Bewegung:
Gemischte Fliess- und Staublawine.
Zunehmende Zertrümmerung von Schnee-
schollen.
Weitere Merkmale: Trockenschneelawine.
Code: C1, E7 oder 0010 7000.
Ort: Col du Lautaret, Frankreich.

Photograph: L. Rey, France.

E. Form of movement
E. Type de mouvement
E. Forma de movimiento
E. Тип движения
E. Form der Bewegung

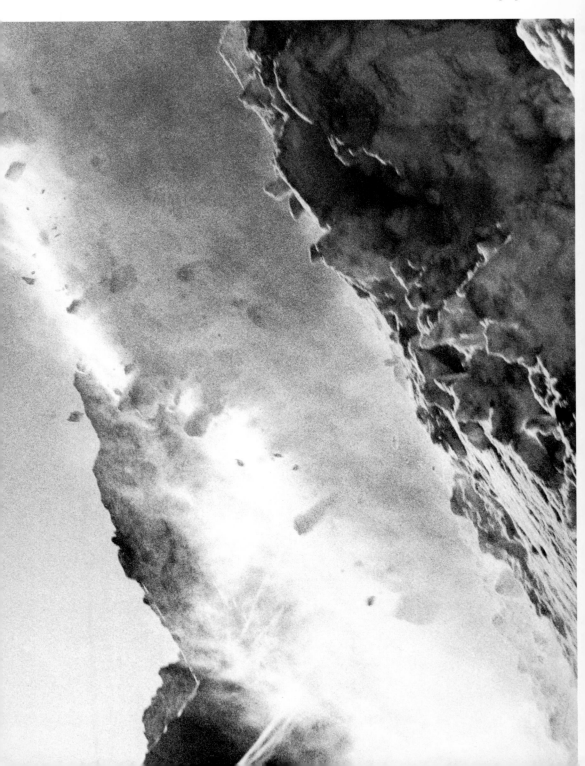

Morphological classification of avalanches
Classification morphologique des avalanches
Clasificación morfológica de las avalanchas
Морфологическая классификация лавин
Morphologische Lawinenklassifikation

182

FIG. 32
Form of movement:
Combined powder and flow avalanche
(indirect evidence). Witness for flow
component: streamlines in the channels;
for powder component: widespread
destruction in the adjacent forest zones.
Code: C1, D2, E7 or 0012 7000.
Location: Hollingergraben, Innsbruck,
Austria.

Type de mouvement:
Avalanche combinée poudreuse et coulante
(d'après des indices indirects). Preuve de la
composante coulante: cannelures dans les
couloirs. Preuve de la composante poudreuse: destruction de larges surfaces dans
les zones forestières avoisinantes.
Code: C1, D2, E7 ou 0012 7000.
Lieu: Hollingergraben, Innsbruck, Autriche.

Forma de movimiento:
Avalancha combinada de polvo y flujo
(evidencia indirecta). Testigo para la
componente de flujo: líneas perfiladas en los
canales. Para componentes de polvo: amplia
destrucción en las zonas forestales contiguas.
Código: C1, D2, E7 o 0012 7000.
Lugar: Hollingergraben, Innsbruck, Austria.

Тип движения:
Комбинированная пылевая и текучая лавина
(косвенные свидетельства). Указания на
текучую компоненту – линии тока в русле,
на пылевую – зона разрушения в приле-
гающем лесу.
Код: C 1, D 2, E 7   Или: 0012, 7000
Район: Холлингерграбен, Иннсбрук,
Австрия

Form der Bewegung:
Gemischte Staub- und Fliesslawine (indirekte
Anzeichen). Anzeichen für den Fliessanteil:
Strömungslinien in den Rinnen; für den
Staubanteil: flächige Zerstörungen in den
seitlich anschliessenden Waldstreifen.
Code: C1, D2, E7 oder 0012 7000.
Ort: Hollingergraben, Innsbruck, Österreich.

Photograph: Alpine Luftbild, Austria
(release by BM.f.LV under No. 13122).

E. *Form of movement*
E. *Type de mouvement*
E. *Forma de movimiento*
E. *Тип движения*
E. *Form der Bewegung*

Morphological classification of avalanches
Classification morphologique des avalanches
Clasificación morfológica de las avalanchas
Морфологическая классификация лавин
Morphologische Lawinenklassifikation

184

FIG. 33
Form of movement:
Flow component of mixed powder/flow
avalanche.
Other characteristics: Dry-slab avalanche.
Channelled zone of transition. Clean, dry
deposit in rounded clods. (The powder
component left the channel at the bend,
escaping to the left of the gully.)
Code: A2, B0, C1, D2, E7, F3, G1, H1
or 2012 7311.
Location: Twin Lakes, Colorado,
United States.

Type de mouvement:
Composante coulante d'une avalanche mixte
poudreuse/coulante.
Autres caractéristiques: Avalanche de
plaque sèche. Zone de transition en couloir.
Dépôt en boules arrondies, propres, sèches.
(La composante poudreuse a quitté le couloir
dans la courbe, s'échappant vers la gauche
du couloir.)
Code: A2, B0, C1, D2, E7, F3, G1, H1
ou 2012 7311.
Lieu: Twin Lakes, Colorado,
Etats-Unis d'Amérique.

Forma de movimiento:
Componente de flujo de una avalancha mixta
de polvo/flujo.
Otras características: avalancha de placa seca.
Zona canalizada de transición. Depósito
limpio y seco en fragmentos redondeados.
(La componente de polvo se salió del canal
en la curva, escapando hacia la izquierda
de la hondonada.)
Código: A2, B0, C1, D2, E7, F3, G1, H1
o 2012 7311.
Lugar: Twin Lakes, Colorado,
Estados Unidos.

Тип движения:
Текучая компонента смешанной текучей и
пылевой лавины.
Другие характеристики: Лавина из сухих
снежных досок. Канализованная зона
транзита. Чистые сухие отложения в виде
окатанных комьев (пылевая составляющая
отложилась на изгибе русла на его левом
борту).
Код: A 2, B 0, C 1, D 2, E 7, F 3, G 1, H 1
Или: 2012, 7311
Район: Твин-Лейкс, Колорадо, США

Form der Bewegung:
Fliessanteil einer gemischten Staub- und
Fliesslawine.
Weitere Merkmale: Trockene Schneebrett-
lawine. Runsenlawine in der Sturzbahn.
Reine, trockene Ablagerung in runden
Knollen. (Der Staubanteil verliess die Runse
an der Biegung und brach nach links aus.)
Code: A2, B0, C1, D2, E7, F3, G1, H1
oder 2012 7311.
Ort: Twin Lakes, Colorado, U.S.A.

Photograph: H. Frutiger, EISLF.

E. Form of movement
E. Type de mouvement
E. Forma de movimiento
E. Тип движения
E. Form der Bewegung

Morphological classification of avalanches
Classification morphologique des avalanches
Clasificación morfológica de las avalanchas
Морфологическая классификация лавин
Morphologische Lawinenklassifikation

186

FIG. 34
Form of movement:
Pure flow avalanche, seen in the direction of flow (sharp change of direction indicates slow motion).
Other characteristics: Wet, channelled avalanche with coarse, wet, clean deposit.
Code: C2, D2, E2, F3, G2, H1 or 0022 2321.
Location: Wolfgang/Davos, Switzerland.

Type de mouvement:
Avalanche coulante pure vue dans la direction du mouvement (le brusque changement de direction indique un mouvement lent).
Autres caractéristiques: Avalanche humide de couloir, avec dépôt grossier, humide et propre.
Code: C2, D2, E2, F3, G2, H1 ou 0022 2321.
Lieu: Wolfgang/Davos, Suisse.

Forma de movimiento:
Avalancha de flujo puro, vista en la dirección del flujo (el cambio brusco de dirección indica movimiento lento).
Otras características: Avalancha húmeda y acanalada, con depósito grueso, húmedo y limpio.
Código: C2, D2, E2, F3, G2, H1 o 0022 2321.
Lugar: Wolfgang/Davos, Suiza.

Тип движения:
Чисто текучая лавина, вид в направлении течения (резкие изменения направления указывают на медленный характер течения).
Другие характеристики: Канализованная лавина из мокрого снега с крупнокомковатыми, мокрыми, чистыми отложениями.
Код: С 2, D 2, E 2, F 3, G 2, H 1
Или: 0022, 2321
Район: Вольфганг/Давос, Швейцария

Form der Bewegung:
Fliesslawine. Blick in Fliessrichtung. (Scharfer Richtungswechsel weist auf langsame Bewegung.)
Weitere Merkmale: Nasse Runsenlawine mit grober, nasser, reiner Ablagerung.
Code: C2, D2, E2, F3, G2, H1 oder 0022 2321.
Ort: Wolfgang/Davos, Schweiz.

Photograph: E. Wengi, EISLF.

E. Form of movement
E. Type de mouvement
E. Forma de movimiento
E. Тип движения
E. Form der Bewegung

Morphological classification of avalanches
Classification morphologique des avalanches
Clasificación morfológica de las avalanchas
Морфологическая классификация лавин
Morphologische Lawinenklassifikation

188

FIG. 35
Form of movement:
Flow avalanche. The cloud development
is not a real powder component. It is
composed of wet snow, temporarily dis-
persed by the cascade.
Code: C2, E2 or 0020 2000.
Location: Zermatt, Switzerland.

Type de mouvement:
Avalanche coulante. Le nuage n'est pas
une véritable composante poudreuse.
Il est constitué de neige humide, tempo-
rairement dispersée par la cascade.
Code: C2, E2 ou 0020 2000.
Lieu: Zermatt, Suisse.

Forma de movimiento:
Avalancha de flujo. La nube no es una
verdadera componente de polvo. Está
compuesta de nieve húmeda, dispersada
temporalmente por la cascada.
Código: C2, E2 o 0020 2000.
Lugar: Zermatt, Suiza.

Тип движения:
Текучая лавина. Развитие снежного облака
не является результатом образования
пылевой составляющей, это следствие
выброса мокрого снега на ступенчатых
обрывах.
Код: С 2, Е 2   Или: 0020, 2000
Район: Церматт, Швейцария

Form der Bewegung:
Fliesslawine. Die Wolkenbildung stellt
keinen eigentlichen Staubanteil dar; sie
besteht aus nassem im Steilabsturz vorüber-
gehend zerstäubtem Schnee.
Code: C2, E2 oder 0020 2000.
Ort: Zermatt, Schweiz.

Photograph: Perren, Switzerland.

E. Form of movement
E. Type de mouvement
E. Forma de movimiento
E. Тип движения
E. Form der Bewegung

Morphological classification of avalanches
Classification morphologique des avalanches
Clasificación morfológica de las avalanchas
Морфологическая классификация лавин
Morphologische Lawinenklassifikation

190

FIG. 36
Surface roughness of deposit:
Fine deposit.
Other characteristics: Dry surface-layer
loose snow avalanches. New-snow fracture,
partly channelled flow. Dry, clean
deposit.
Code: A1, B2, C1, D7, E2, F4, G1, H1
or 1217 2411.
Location: Schafläger, Davos, Switzerland.

Rugosité superficielle du dépôt:
Dépôt fin.
Autres caractéristiques: Avalanches superficielles de neige sans cohésion. Cassure
dans la neige fraîche, avalanche coulante
partiellement canalisée. Dépôt sec et
propre.
Code: A1, B2, C1, D7, E2, F4, G1, H1
ou 1217 2411.
Lieu: Schafläger, Davos, Suisse.

Rugosidad superficial del depósito:
Depósito fino.
Otras características: avalanchas de capa
superficial seca y de nieve suelta. Fractura de
nieve nueva; flujo parcialmente canalizado.
Depósito limpio y seco.
Código: A1, B2, C1, D7, E2, F4, G1, H1
o 1217 2411.
Lugar: Schafläger, Davos, Suiza.

Поверхностная шероховатость отложений:
Мелкокомковатые отложения.
Другие характеристики: Лавина повер-
хностного слоя из сухого рыхлого снега.
Плоскость срыва в новом снегу, текучая
частично канализованная лавина. Сухие
чистые отложения.
Код: A 1, B 2, C 1, D 7, E 2, F 4, G 1, H 1
Или: 1217, 2411
Район: Шафлегер, Давос, Швейцария

Oberflächenrauhigkeit der Ablagerung:
Feine Ablagerung.
Weitere Merkmale: Trockene Lockerschnee-
lawinen. Oberlawinen mit Neuschneebruch.
Fliesslawinen, teilweise Runsenlawinen.
Trockene, reine Ablagerung.
Code: A1, B2, C1, D7, E2, F4, G1, H1
oder 1217 2411.
Ort: Schafläger, Davos, Schweiz.

Photograph: E. Wengi, EISLF.

F. Surface roughness of deposit
F. Rugosité superficielle du dépôt
F. Rugosidad superficial del depósito
F. Поверхностная шероховатость отложений
F. Oberflächenrauhigkeit der Ablagerung

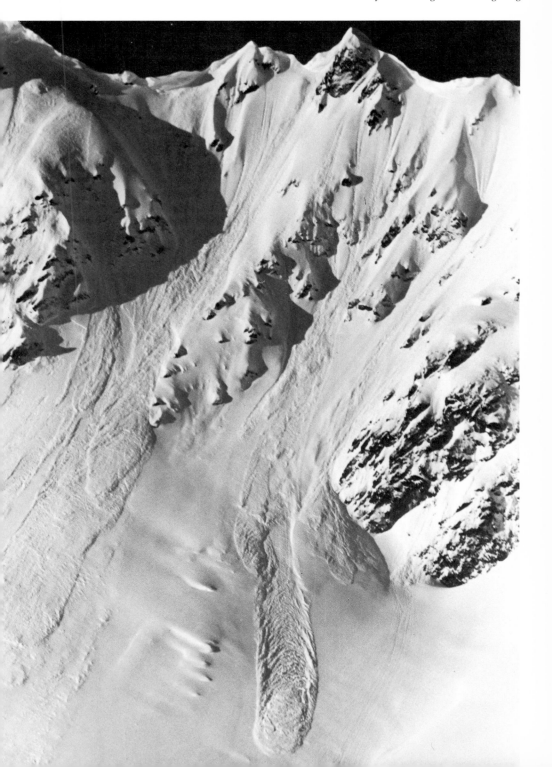

Morphological classification of avalanches
Classification morphologique des avalanches
Clasificación morfológica de las avalanchas
Морфологическая классификация лавин
Morphologische Lawinenklassifikation

192

FIG. 37
Surface roughness of deposit:
Coarse deposit in angular blocks.
Other characteristics: Clean dry deposit of
a hard slab avalanche, flowing along the
ground.
Code: A4, B0, C1, D0, E2, F2, G1, H1
or 4010 2211.

Rugosité superficielle du dépôt:
Dépôt grossier en blocs anguleux.
Autres caractéristiques: dépôt propre et sec
issu d'une avalanche de plaque dure, coulant
le long du sol.
Code: A4, B0, C1, D0, E2, F2, G1, H1
ou 4010 2211.

Rugosidad superficial del depósito:
Depósito grueso en bloques angulosos.
Otras características: depósito limpio y seco
de una avalancha de placa dura, que fluye a lo
largo del suelo.
Código: A4, B0, C1, D0, E2, F2, G1, H1
o 4010 2211.

Поверхностная шероховатость отложений:
Крупнокомковатые отложения из
угловатых глыб.
Другие характеристики: Чистые сухие
отложения текучей лавины из твердых
снежных досок.
Код: A 4, B 0, C 1, D 0, E 2, G 1, H 1
Или: 4010, 2211.

Oberflächenrauhigkeit der Ablagerung:
Grobe Ablagerung in kantigen Schollen.
Weitere Merkmale: Reine, trockene Abla-
gerung einer harten, dem Boden folgenden
Schneebrettlawine.
Code: A4, B0, C1, D0, E2, F2, G1, H1
oder 4010 2211.

Photograph: E. Wengi, EISLF.

F. *Surface roughness of deposit*
F. *Rugosité superficielle du dépôt*
F. *Rugosidad superficial del depósito*
F. *Поверхностная шероховатость отложений*
F. *Oberflächenrauhigkeit der Ablagerung*

Morphological classification of avalanches
Classification morphologique des avalanches
Clasificación morfológica de las avalanchas
Морфологическая классификация лавин
Morphologische Lawinenklassifikation

194

FIG. 38
Surface roughness of deposit:
Coarse deposit in rounded clods.
Other characteristics: Wet channelled flow
avalanche with wet clean deposit (direction
of flow ↓).
Code: D2, E2, F3, G2, H1 or 0002 2321.

Rugosité superficielle du dépôt:
Dépôt grossier en boules arrondies.
Autres caractéristiques: Avalanche de
couloir coulante, humide, avec dépôt propre
et humide (direction de l'écoulement ↓).
Code: D2, E2, F3, G2, H1 ou 0002 2321.

Rugosidad superficial del depósito:
Depósito grueso en fragmentos redondeados.
Otras características: avalancha de flujo
acanalada húmeda con depósito limpio y
húmedo (dirección del flujo ↓).
Código: D2, E2, F3, G2, H1 o 0002 2321.

Поверхностная шероховатость отложений:
Крупнокомковатые отложения из окатанных комьев.
Другие характеристики: Канализованная
текучая лавина из мокрого снега с мокрыми
чистыми отложениями (направление
течения ↓)
Код: D 2, E 2, F 3, C 2, H 1
Или: 0002, 2321

Oberflächenrauhigkeit der Ablagerung:
Grobe Ablagerung in runden Knollen.
Weitere Merkmale: Nasse Runsenlawine.
Fliesslawine mit nasser, reiner Ablagerung
(Fliessrichtung ↓).
Code: D2, E2, F3, G2, H1 oder 0002 2321.

Photograph: M. Shoda, Japan.

F. Surface roughness of deposit
F. Rugosité superficielle du dépôt
F. Rugosidad superficial del depósito
F. Поверхностная шероховатость отложений
F. Oberflächenrauhigkeit der Ablagerung

Morphological classification of avalanches
Classification morphologique des avalanches
Clasificación morfológica de las avalanchas
Морфологическая классификация лавин
Morphologische Lawinenklassifikation

196

FIG. 39
Surface roughness of deposit:
Deposit in rounded clods (particular formation probably due to mixture of dry and wet snow).
Other characteristics: Channelled flow avalanche, slight contamination.
Code: D2, E2, F3, G2, H2 or 0002 2322.

Rugosité superficielle du dépôt:
Dépôts en boules arrondies (formation particulière, probablement due au mélange de neige sèche et humide).
Autres caractéristiques: Avalanche coulante de couloir, légèrement souillée.
Code: D2, E2, F3, G2, H2 ou 0002 2322.

Rugosidad superficial del depósito:
Depósito en fragmentos redondeados (formación particular debida probablemente a la mezcla de nieve seca y húmeda).
Otras características: avalancha de flujo acanalada, ligera contaminación.
Código: D2, E2, F3, G2, H2 o 0002 2322.

Поверхностная шероховатсть отложений:
Отложения из окатанных комьев (эти образования вероятно обусловлены смесью сухого и мокрого снега).
Другие характеристики: Канализованная текучая лавина, слегка загрязненные отложения.
Код: D 2, E 2, F 3, G 2, H 2
Или: 0002, 2322

Oberflächenrauhigkeit der Ablagerung:
Ablagerung in runden Knollen. (Besondere Bildung wahrscheinlich verursacht durch die Mischung von trockenem und nassem Schnee.)
Weitere Merkmale: Runsenlawine, Fliesslawine, schwach verunreinigt.
Code: D2, E2, F3, G2, H2 oder 0002 2322.

Photograph: E. Sommerhalder, EISLF.

197

F. *Surface roughness of deposit*
F. *Rugosité superficielle du dépôt*
F. *Rugosidad superficial del depósito*
F. *Поверхностная шероховатость отложений*
F. *Oberflächenrauhigkeit der Ablagerung*

Morphological classification of avalanches
Classification morphologique des avalanches
Clasificación morfológica de las avalanchas
Морфологическая классификация лавин
Morphologische Lawinenklassifikation

198

FIG. 40
Liquid water in snow debris at time of deposition:
Absent (dry avalanche deposit).
Soft dry-slab avalanche.
Other characteristics: Surface-layer (new snow), unconfined flow avalanche; fine, dry clean deposit.
Code: A3, B2, C1, D1, E2, F4, G1, H1 or 3211 2411.
Location: Alta, Utah, United States.

Eau liquide dans la neige au moment du dépôt:
Absente (dépôt sec).
Avalanche de plaque tendre sèche.
Autres caractéristiques: Avalanche de versant coulante, superficielle (dans la neige fraîche); dépôt fin, sec et propre.
Code: A3, B2, C1, D1, E2, F4, G1, H1 ou 3211 2411.
Lieu: Alta, Utah, Etats-Unis d'Amérique.

Agua líquida en los desechos de la nieve en el momento del depósito:
Ausente (depósito de avalancha seca).
Avalancha de placa seca y blanda.
Otras características: avalancha de flujo sin confinar, de capa superficial (nieve nueva); depósito fino, seco y limpio.
Código: A3, B2, C1, D1, E2, F4, G1, H1 o 3211 2411.
Lugar: Alta, Utah, Estados Unidos.

Жидкая вода в снежных отложениях во время остановки:
Отсутствует (сухие лавинные отложения). Сухая лавина поверхностного слоя из мягкой снежной доски.
Другие харктеристики: Канализованная текучая лавина, мелкокомковатый сухой, чистый снег в зоне отложения.
Код: А 3, В 2, С 1, D 1, E 2, F 4, G 1, H 1
Или: 3211, 2411
Район: Альта, Юта, США.

Flüssiges Wasser in Ablagerung:
Fehlend (trocken). Trockene Ablagerung.
Trockene weiche Schneebrettlawine.
Weitere Merkmale: Oberlawine, Neuschneebruch, Flächenlawine, Fliesslawine mit feiner, trockener, reiner Ablagerung.
Code: A3, B2, C1, D1, E2, F4, G1, H1 oder 3211 2411.
Ort: Alta, Utah, U.S.A.

Photograph: E. R. LaChapelle, United States.

G. Liquid water in snow debris
G. Eau liquide dans la neige
G. Agua líquida en los desechos de la nieve
G. Жидкая вода в снежных отложениях во время остановки
G. Flüssiges Wasser in Ablagerung

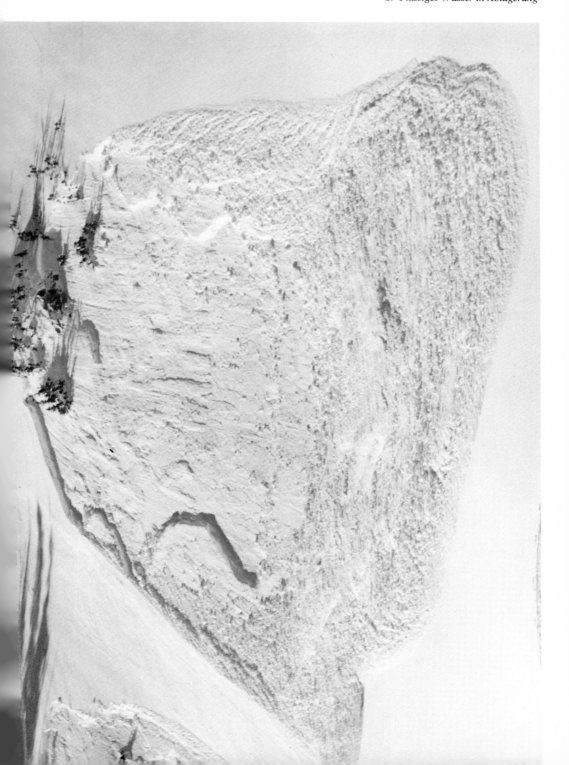

Morphological classification of avalanches
Classification morphologique des avalanches
Clasificación morfológica de las avalanchas
Морфологическая классификация лавин
Morphologische Lawinenklassifikation

200

F_IG. 41
Liquid water in snow debris at time of deposition:
Present (wet avalanche deposit).
Coarse deposit in rounded clods.
Other characteristics: Wet slab (fracture just visible), channelled flow avalanche with partly contaminated wet deposit. (The classic term 'ground avalanche' is appropriate to this combination of features.)
Code: A2, B0, C2, D2, E2, F3, G2, H7 or 2022 2327.
Location: Davos-Glaris, Switzerland.

Eau liquide dans la neige au moment du dépôt:
Présente (dépôt humide).
Dépôt grossier en boules arrondies.
Autres caractéristiques: Avalanche de plaque humide (cassure juste visible). Avalanche coulante de couloir avec dépôt humide partiellement souillée. (Le terme classique «avalanche terrière» correspond bien à cette combinaison de caractères.)
Code: A2, B0, C2, D2, E2, F3, G2, H7 ou 2022 2327.
Lieu: Davos-Glaris, Suisse.

Agua líquida en los desechos de la nieve en el momento del depósito:
Presente (depósito húmedo).
Depósito grueso en fragmentos redondeados.
Otras características: avalancha de placa húmeda (la fractura es apenas visible). Avalancha de flujo acanalada con depósito húmedo parcialmente contaminado. (El término clásico de «avalancha de tierra» es apropiado para esta combinación de características.)
Código: A2, B0, C2, D2, E2, F3, G2, H7 o 2022 2327.
Lugar: Davos-Glaris, Suiza.

Жидкая вода в снежных отложениях во время остановки:
Имеется (мокрые лавинные отложения). Крупнокомковатые отложения из окатанных комьев.
Другие характеристики: Мокрая лавина из снежных досок (видна поверхность скольжения). Канализованная текучая лавина с частично загряненными мокрыми отложеннями. (Классический термин «грунтовая лавина» хорошо подходит для этой комбинации характеристик лавины.)
Код: А 2, В 0, С 2, D 2, Е 2, F 3, G 2, Н 7 Или: 2022, 2327
Район: Давос-Гларис, Швейцария

Flüssiges Wasser in Ablagerung:
Vorhanden (nass). Nasse (feuchte) Ablagerung.
Grobe Ablagerung in runden Knollen.
Weitere Merkmale: Nasse Schneebrettlawine (Anriss knapp sichtbar). Runsenlawine mit teilweise unreiner Ablagerung. (Für diese Kombination von Merkmalen ist der klassische Begriff der Grundlawine angemessen.)
Code: A2, B0, C2, D2, E2, F3, G2, H7 oder 2022 2327.
Ort: Davos/Glaris, Schweiz.

Photograph: M. Meerkämper, Switzerland.

G. Liquid water in snow debris
G. Eau liquide dans la neige
G. Agua líquida en los desechos de la nieve
G. Жидкая вода в снежных отложениях во время остановки
G. Flüssiges Wasser in Ablagerung

Morphological classification of avalanches
Classification morphologique des avalanches
Clasificación morfológica de las avalanchas
Морфологическая классификация лавин
Morphologische Lawinenklassifikation

202

FIG. 42
Contamination of deposit:
Clean deposit of slab avalanche.
Other characteristics: Mainly fine deposit, some angular blocks indicate the presence of hard slabs.
Code: F7, G1, H1 or 2000 2711.

Souillure du dépôt:
Dépôt propre d'une avalanche de plaque.
Autres caractéristiques: Dépôt surtout fin; quelques blocs anguleux révèlent la présence de plaques dures.
Code: F7, G1, H1 ou 2000 2711.

Contaminación del depósito:
Depósito limpio de una avalancha de placa.
Otras características: depósito principalmente fino, algunos bloques angulosos indican la presencia de placas duras.
Código: F7, G1, H1 o 2000 2711.

Загрязнение отложений:
Чистые отложения лавины из снежных досок
Другие характериктики: Большею частью отложения мелкокомковатые, некоторые угловатые блоки указывают на твердую снежную доску.
Код: F 7, G 1, H 1   Или: 2000, 2711

Fremdmaterial in der Ablagerung:
Reine Ablagerung einer Schneebrettlawine.
Weitere Merkmale: Grösstenteils feine Ablagerung, einige kantige Blöcke weisen auf eine harte Schneebrettlawine.
Code: F7, G1, H1 oder 2000 2711.

Photograph: E. Wengi, EISLF.

203

H. *Contamination of deposit*
H. *Souillure du dépôt*
H. *Contaminación del depósito*
H. *Загрязнение отложений*
H. *Fremdmaterial in der Ablagerung*

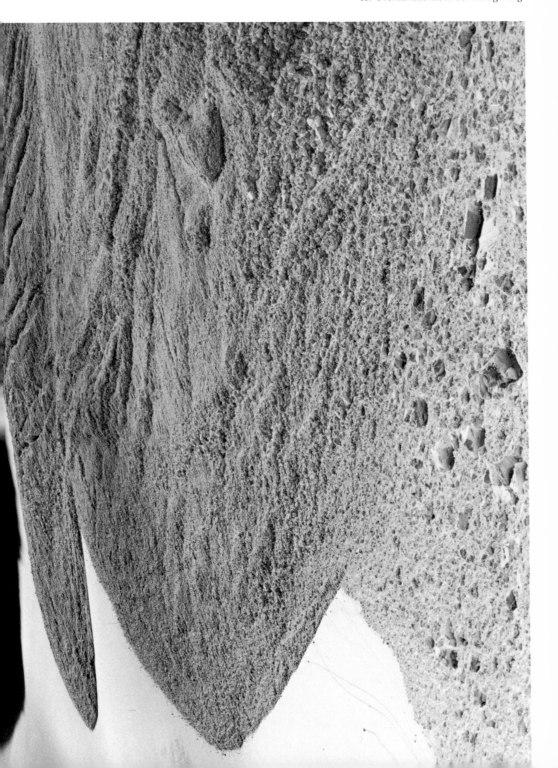

Morphological classification of avalanches
Classification morphologique des avalanches
Clasificación morfológica de las avalanchas
Морфологическая классификация лавин
Morphologische Lawinenklassifikation

FIG. 43
Contamination of deposit:
Centre: Contaminated deposit (debris).
Left and right: clean deposits.
Other characteristics:
Centre: Channelled wet flow avalanche with coarse, wet deposit (crow-foot type).
Code: D2, E2, F3, G2, H3 or 0002 2323.
Left: Wet unconfined surface-layer loose snow avalanche. Flow avalanche with coarse, clean, wet deposit.
Code: A1, B1, C2, D1, E2, F1, G2, H1 or 1121 2121.
Right: Unconfined surface-layer slab avalanche; flow avalanche with coarse, clean deposit (moisture conditions not apparent).
Code: A2, B0, C0, D1, E2, F1, G0, H1 or 2001 2101.

Souillure du dépôt:
Au centre: dépôt souillé (débris). *A gauche* et *à droite:* dépôts propres.
Autres caractéristiques:
Au centre: avalanche coulante humide de couloir avec dépôt humide et grossier (du type patte d'oie).
Code: D2, E2, F3, G2, H3 ou 0002 2323.
A gauche: Avalanche superficielle de versant, de neige humide sans cohésion.
Avalanche coulante avec dépôt humide, propre et grossier.
Code: A1, B1, C2, D1, E2, F1, G2, H1 ou 1121 2121.
A droite: Avalanche superficielle de versant; avalanche coulante de plaque avec dépôt propre et grossier (aucun signe visible d'humidité).
Code: A2, B0, C0, D1, E2, F1, G0, H1 ou 2001 2101.

Contaminación del depósito:
Centro: depósito contaminado (escombros).
Izquierda y derecha: depósitos limpios.
Otras características:
Centro: avalancha húmeda de flujo acanalada con depósito grueso y húmedo (tipo pata de cuervo).
Código: D2, E2, F3, G2, H3 o 0002 2323.
Izquierda: avalancha de nieve suelta de capa superficial sin confinar y húmeda; avalancha de flujo con depósito grueso, limpio y húmedo.

Código: A1, B1, C2, D1, E2, F1, G2, H1 o 1121 2121.
Derecha: avalancha superficial de placa sin confinar; avalancha de flujo con depósito limpio y grueso (ningún indicio de humedad).
Código: A2, B0, C0, D1, E2, F1, G0, H1 o 2001 2101.

Загрязнение отложений:
Центр: загрязненные отложения (обломки).
Слева и справа чистые отложения.
Другие характеристики: В центре: канализованная текучая лавина из мокрого снега с крупнокомковатыми мокрыми отложениями (похожа на след вороны).
Код: D 2, E 2, F 3, C 2, H 3
Или: 0002, 2323
Слева: Неканализованная лавина поверхностного слоя из мокрого рыхлого снега. Текучая лавина с крупнокомковатыми чистыми мокрыми отлсжениями.
Код: A 1, B 1, C 1, Д 1, E 2, 0 1, Д 2, H 1
Или: 1121, 2121
Справа: неканализованиая лавина поверхностного слоя из снежных досок.
Текучая лавина с крупнокомковатыми чистыми отложениями (увлаженения не видно)
Код: A 2, B 0, C 0, D 1, E 2, F 1, G 0, H 1
Или: 2001, 2101

Fremdmaterial in der Ablagerung:
Mitte: Unreine Ablagerung (Erdmaterial).
Links und rechts: Reine Ablagerungen.
Weitere Merkmale:
Mitte: Nasse Runsenlawine, Fliesslawine mit grober, nasser Ablagerung (Krähenfusstyp).
Code: D2, E2, F3, G2, H3 oder 0002 2323.
Links: Nasse Lockerschneelawine, Flächenlawine, Oberlawine, mit grober, reiner, nasser Ablagerung.
Code: A1, B1, C2, D1, E2, F1, G2, H1 oder 1121 2121.
Rechts: Schneebrettlawine, Flächenlawine, Oberlawine, Fliesslawine (Feuchteverhältnisse nicht erkennbar).
Code: A2, B0, C0, D1, E2, F1, G0, H1 oder 2001 2101.

Photograph: M. Shoda, Japan.

H. Contamination of deposit
H. Souillure du dépôt
H. Contaminación del depósito
Н. Загрязнение отложений
H. Fremdmaterial in der Ablagerung

Morphological classification of avalanches
Classification morphologique des avalanches
Clasificación morfológica de las avalanchas
Морфологическая классификация лавин
Morphologische Lawinenklassifikation

206

FIG. 44
Contamination of deposit:
Heavily contaminated wet deposit (debris, soil, branches) several months after the event. Owing to snow melt, dirt is concentrated at the surface. View in direction of avalanche flow.
Other characteristics: Channelled flow avalanche.
Code: D2, E2, F0, G2, H8 or 0002 2028.
Location: Mt. Mitsumine, Shiretoko Peninsula, Hokkaido, Japan.

Souillure du dépôt:
Dépôt humide lourdement souillé (débris, terre, branches) plusieurs mois après l'événement. En raison de la fusion de la neige, la saleté est concentrée à la surface. Vue dans la direction de l'avalanche.
Autres caractéristiques: Avalanche coulante de couloir.
Code: D2, E2, F0, G2, H8 ou 0002 2028.
Lieu: Mt. Mitsumine Shiretoko Peninsula, Hokkaido, Japon.

Contaminación del depósito:
Depósito húmedo fuertemente contaminado (escombros, tierra, ramas), varios meses después del incidente. Debido a la fusión de la nieve, la tierra está concentrada en la superficie. Visto en la dirección del flujo de la avalancha.
Otras características: avalancha de flujo acanalada.
Código: D2, E2, F0, G2, H8 o 0002 2028.
Lugar: Mt. Mitsumine, Península de Shiretoko, Hokkaido, Japón.

Загрязнение отложений:
Сильно загрязненные мокрые отложения (обломки, почва, ветки) через несколько месяцев после схода лавины. В результате таяния загрязнение сконцентрировалось на поверхности. Вид в направлении течения.
Другие характеристики: Канализованная текучая лавина.
Код: D 2, E 2, F 0, G 2, H 8
Или: 0002, 2029
Район: Гора Мицумине, полуостров Ширетоко, Хоккайдо, Япония

Fremdmaterial in der Ablagerung:
Hochgradig unreine nasse Ablagerung (Schutt, Erdmaterial, Äste) einige Monate nach dem Niedergang. Infolge des Schmelzens hat sich das Fremdmaterial an der Oberfläche angereichert. Blick in der Fliessrichtung der Lawine.
Weitere Merkmale: Runsenlawine, Fliesslawine.
Code: D2, E2, F0, G2, H8 oder 0002 2028.
Ort: Mt. Mitsumine, Shiretoko-Halbinsel, Hokkaido, Japan.

Photograph: H. Onodera, Japan.

H. Contamination of deposit
H. Souillure du dépôt
H. Contaminación del depósito
Н. Загрязнение отложений
H. Fremdmaterial in der Ablagerung

Morphological classification of avalanches
Classification morphologique des avalanches
Clasificación morfológica de las avalanchas
Морфологическая классификация лавин
Morphologische Lawinenklassifikation

208

FIG. 45
Contamination of deposit:
Deposit contaminated by soil and timber.
Other characteristics: Dry, unconfined mixed flow and powder avalanche.
Code: C1, D1, E7, F0, G1, H8 or 0011 7018.
Location: Vinadi, Engadine, Switzerland.

Souillure du dépôt:
Dépôt souillé par de la terre et du bois.
Autres caractéristiques: Avalanche sèche de versant, mixte coulante et poudreuse.
Code: C1, D1, E7, F0, G1, H8 ou 0011 7018.
Lieu: Vinadi, Engadine, Suisse.

Contaminación del depósito:
Depósito contaminado con tierra y madera.
Otras características: avalancha seca sin confinar, de polvo y de flujo mixto.
Código: C1, D1, E7, F0, G1, H8 o 0011 7018.
Lugar: Vinadi, Engadine, Suiza.

Загрязнение отложений:
Отложения загрязненные остатками почвы и леса
Другие характеристики: Неканализован-
ная смешанная текучая и пылевая лавина из сухого снега.
Код: C 1, D 1, E 7, F 0, G 1, H 8
Или: 0011, 7018
Район: Винади, Энгадин, Швейцария

Fremdmaterial in der Ablagerung:
Ablagerung durchsetzt von Erdmaterial und Bäumen.
Weitere Merkmale: Trockene, gemischte Fliess- und Staublawine. Flächenlawine.
Code: C1, D1, E7, F0, G1, H8
oder 0011 7018.
Ort: Vinadi, Engadin, Schweiz.

Photograph: H. in der Gand, EISLF.

H. Contamination of deposit
H. Souillure du dépôt
H. Contaminación del depósito
Н. Загрязнение отложений
H. Fremdmaterial in der Ablagerung

Morphological classification of avalanches
Classification morphologique des avalanches
Clasificación morfológica de las avalanchas
Морфологическая классификация лавин
Morphologische Lawinenklassifikation

210

FIG. 46
Contamination of deposit:
Deposit 'contaminated' with timber after partial melting.
Code: H4.
Location: Pignia, Grisons, Switzerland.

Souillure du dépôt:
Dépôt «souillé» par du bois après fusion partielle.
Code: H4.
Lieu: Pignia, Grisons, Suisse.

Contaminación del depósito:
Depósito «contaminado» con madera después de la fusión parcial.
Código: H4.
Lugar: Pignia, Grisons, Suiza.

Загрязнение отложений:
Отложения, «загрязненные» лесом, после частичного таяния.
Код: Н 4
Район: Пигния, Гризонс, Швейцария

Fremdmaterial in der Ablagerung:
Ablagerung durchsetzt von Baumtrümmern nach teilweiser Schneeschmelze.
Code: H4.
Ort: Pignia, Graubünden, Schweiz.

Photograph: H. Etter, EISLF.

H. *Contamination of deposit*
H. *Souillure du dépôt*
H. *Contaminación del depósito*
Н. *Загрязнение отложений*
H. *Fremdmaterial in der Ablagerung*

Morphological classification of avalanches
Classification morphologique des avalanches
Clasificación morfológica de las avalanchas
Морфологическая классификация лавин
Morphologische Lawinenklassifikation

212

FIG. 47
Contamination of deposit:
Snow deposit mingled with debris of structures (houses, stables).
Code: H5 or 0000 0005.

Souillure du dépôt:
Dépôt de neige mêlé avec des débris d'ouvrages (maisons, étables).
Code: H5 ou 0000 0005.

Contaminación del depósito:
Depósito de nieve mezclado con escombros de estructuras (casas, establos).
Código: H5 o 0000 0005.

Загрязнение отложений:
Отложения лавины смешанные с обломками сооружений (ломов и конюшен).
Код: Н 5 Или: 0000, 0005

Fremdmaterial in der Ablagerung:
Ablagerung durchsetzt mit Gebäudetrümmern (Häuser, Ställe).
Code: H5 oder 0000 0005.

Photograph: ATP Bilderdienst, Switzerland.

H. *Contamination of deposit*
H. *Souillure du dépôt*
H. *Contaminación del depósito*
Н. *Загрязнение отложений*
H. *Fremdmaterial in der Ablagerung*

2 Snow types and stratification
Types de neige et stratification
Tipos de nieve y estratificación
Типы снега и стратиграфия
Schneearten und Schneeschichtung

Snow types and stratification
Types de neige et stratification
Tipos de nieve y estratificación
Типы снега: Стратиграфия
Schneearten und Schneeschichtung

216

FIG. 48 a, b
Type of snow:
Crystals and grains of snow deposit detached
from the natural structure. (A grain is a
visible unit of one or several crystals.)
Scale: 2 mm.
(a) Dendritic new-snow crystals (stars).
Snow classification: Fa (or F1), D 2.5 (mm).
(b) Partly branched crystals. Intermediate
stage between new snow and old snow. Felt-
like structure.
Snow classification: Fb (or F2), D 1.5 (mm).

Type de neige:
Cristaux et grains de neige déposée détachés
de la structure naturelle (grain = unité visible
d'un ou de plusieurs cristaux).
Echelle: 2 mm.
(a) Cristaux de neige fraîche à dendrites
(étoiles).
Classification de la neige: Fa (ou F1),
D 2,5 (mm).
(b) Cristaux partiellement ramifiés. Stade
intermédiaire entre neige fraîche et vieille
neige. Structure feutrée.
Classification de la neige: Fb (ou F2),
D 1,5 (mm).

Tipos de nieve:
Cristales y granos de la nieve depositada
separados de su estructura natural
(grano = unidad visible de uno o varios
cristales).
Escala: 2 mm.
(a) Cristales de nieve nueva dendréticos
(estrellas).
Clasificación de la nieve: Fa (o F1),
D 2,5 (mm).
(b) Cristales parcialmente ramificados. Fase
intermedia entre nieve nueva y nieve vieja.
Estructura como de fieltro.
Clasificación de la nieve: Fb (o F2),
D 1,5 (mm).

Тип снега
Кристаллы и зерна отложенного снега.
Разъединяемые из натуральной связи
(зерно — видимая единица одного или
нескольких кристаллов).
Масштаб 2 мм.
(а) Дендровидные кристаллы нового снега
(звездочки).
Классификация снега: Fa (или F 1), D 2,5 (мм)
(b) Кристаллы частично видоизмененной
структуры Промежуточная стадия между
новым и старым снегом.
Классификация снега: Fb (или F 2), D 1,5 (мм)

Schneearten:
Kristalle und Körner von abgelagertem
Schnee aus dem natürlichen Verband heraus-
gelöst. (Korn = sichtbare Einheit eines oder
mehrerer Kristalle.)
Massstab: 2 mm.
(a) Dendritische (verästelte) Neuschnee-
kristalle (Sterne).
Schneeklassifikation: Fa (oder F1),
D 2,5 (mm).
(b) Teilweise verästelte Kristalle.
Zwischenstadium zwischen Neu- und Alt-
schnee. Filzige Struktur.
Schneeklassifikation: Fb (oder F2),
D 1,5 (mm).

Photograph: E. Wengi, EISLF.

T. Snow types
T. Types de neige
T. Tipos de nieve
Т. Типы снега
T. Schneearten

a

b

Snow types and stratification
Types de neige et stratification
Tipos de nieve y estratificación
Типы снега: Стратиграфия
Schneearten und Schneeschichtung

218

FIG. 48 c, d
Type of snow:
(c) Rounded grains (predominantly destructive metamorphism).
Snow classificaion: Fc (or F3), D 0.7 (mm).
(d) Irregular, mainly faceted grains (under constructive metamorphism).
Snow classification: Fd (or F4), D 1.5 (mm).

Type de neige:
(c) Grains arrondis (dominance de la métamorphose destructrice).
Classification de la neige: Fc (ou F3), D 0,7 (mm).
(d) Grains irréguliers, de préférence anguleux (en état de métamorphose constructrice).
Classification de la neige: Fd (ou F4), D 1,5 (mm).

Tipos de nieve:
(c) Granos redondeados (metamorfismo destructivo dominante).
Clasificación de la nieve: Fc (o F3), D 0,7 (mm).
(d) Granos irregulares, principalmente facetados (en metamorfismo constructivo).
Clasificación de la nieve: Fd (o F4), D 1,5 (mm).

Тип снега
(c) Зерна округлой формы (преобладает деструктивный метаморфизм)
Классификация снега: Fc (или F 3), D 0,7 (мм)
(d) Неправильные, главным образом ограненные зерна (под влиянием конструктивного метаморфизма)
Классификация снега: Fd (или F 4), D 1,5 (мм)

Schneearten:
(c) Gerundete Körner (vorherrschende abbauende Umwandlung).
Schneeklassifikation: Fc (oder F3), D 0,7 (mm).
(d) Unregelmässige, vorwiegend kantige Körner (unter aufbauender Umwandlung).
Schneeklassifikation: Fd (oder F4), D 1,5 (mm).

Photograph: E. Wengi, EISLF.

T. Snow types
T. Types de neige
T. Tipos de nieve
T. Типы снега
T. Schneearten

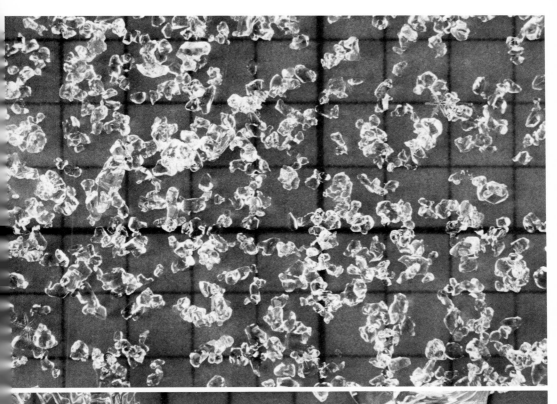

c

d

Snow types and stratification
Types de neige et stratification
Tipos de nieve y estratificación
Типы снега: Стратиграфия
Schneearten und Schneeschichtung

220

FIG. 48 e, f
Type of snow:
(e) Ribbed, partly cup-shaped crystals.
Depth hoar (final state of constructive
metamorphism).
Snow classification: Fe (or F5), D 3 (mm).
(f) Rounded old-snow grains after melt
metamorphism. Strong bonds between
grains are visible.
Snow classification: Fc (or F3), D 2 (mm).

Type de neige:
(e) Cristaux cannelés et gobelets. Givre de
profondeur (stade final de la métamorphose
constructrice).
Classification de la neige: Fe (ou F5),
D 3 (mm).
(f) Grains arrondis de vieille neige après
métamorphose de fonte. Des liaisons fortes
entre plusieurs cristaux sont visibles.
Classification de la neige: Fc (ou F3),
D 2 (mm).

Tipos de nieve:
(e) Cristales en forma de nervios y
parcialmente acopados. Escarcha profunda
(estado final del metamorfismo constructivo).
Clasificación de la nieve: Fe (o F5), D 3 (mm).
(f) Granos de nieve vieja redondeados
después del metamorfismo por fusión.
Resultan visibles fuertes uniones entre los
granos.
Clasificación de la nieve: Fc (o F3), D 2 (mm).

Тип снега
(e) Кристаллы ограненные ребристые,
чашеобразные
Глубинная изморозь (конечная фаза
конструктивного метаморфизма)
(f) Округленные зерна
происходящие в результате таяния.
Заметны прочные связи между кристал-
лами.
Классификация снега: Fc (или F 3), D 2 (мм)

Schneearten:
(e) Geriefte, teilweise becherförmige
Kristalle. Schwimmschnee. (Endstadium der
aufbauenden Umwandlung.)
Schneeklassifikation: Fe (oder F5), D 3 (mm).
(f) Gerundete Altschneekörner nach
Schmelzumwandlung. Starke Bindungen
zwischen Kristallen sind sichtbar.
Schneeklassifikation: Fc (oder F3), D 2 (mm).

Photograph: E. Wengi, EISLF.

T. Snow types
T. Types de neige
T. Tipos de nieve
T. Типы снега
T. Schneearten

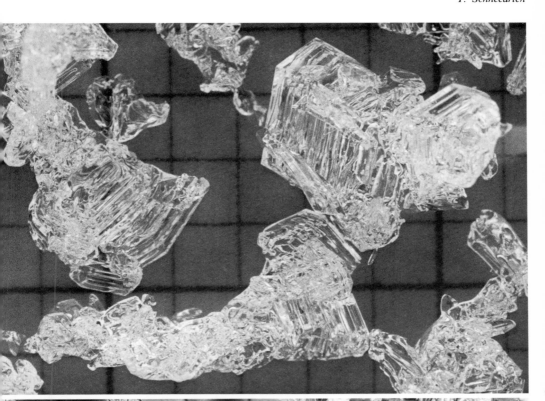

e

f

Snow types and stratification
Types de neige et stratification
Tipos de nieve y estratificación
Типы снега: Стратиграфия
Schneearten und Schneeschichtung

222

FIG. 49
Stratification:
Snow strata: Transparent snow profile (sun shining through thin snow wall). Dark layers: fine, granular, dense snow; mainly destructive metamorphism. Light layers: coarse, granular, rather loose snow; faceted crystals; highly constructive metamorphism. Scale (nails): 10 cm. Central bar: Cone penetrometer.

Stratification:
Couches de neige: Profil de neige par transparence (lumière solaire pénétrant parois de neige mince). Niveaux sombres: neige dense à grains fins; métamorphose principalement destructrice. Niveaux clairs: neige à gros grains assez peu cohérente; cristaux anguleux; forte métamorphose constructrice. Echelle (clous): 10 cm. Au centre, sonde de battage.

Estratificación:
Capas de nieve: perfil de la nieve por transparencia (pared delgada de nieve penetrada por luz solar). Capas oscuras: nieve densa granular y fina: metamorfismo principalmente destructivo. Capas claras: nieve granular gruesa, bastante suelta; cristales facetados; metamorfismo altamente constructivo.
Escala (clavos): 10 cm. Barra central: penetrómetro de cono (ramsonda).

Стратиграфия:
Снежные слои: Разрез снежного покрова в ярком солнечном свете. Темные слои: мелкозернистый плотный снег, сформированный в основном деструктивным метаморфизмом. Светлые слои: крупнозернистый более рыхлый снег, ограненные кристаллы, образован интенсивным конструктивным метаморфизмом. Размер (между точками): 10 см. В центральной полосе конусный пенетрометр.

Schneeschichtung:
Schneeprofil in durchscheinendem Licht. (Sonne scheint durch dünne Schneewand.) Dunkle Schichten: Feinkörniger, dichter Schnee. Vorwiegend abbauende Umwandlung. Helle Schichten: Grobkörniger, eher lockerer Schnee. Kantige Kristalle, starke aufbauende Umwandlung.
Skala (Nägel): 10 cm. Stange in der Mitte: Rammsonde.

Photograph: M. de Quervain, EISLF.

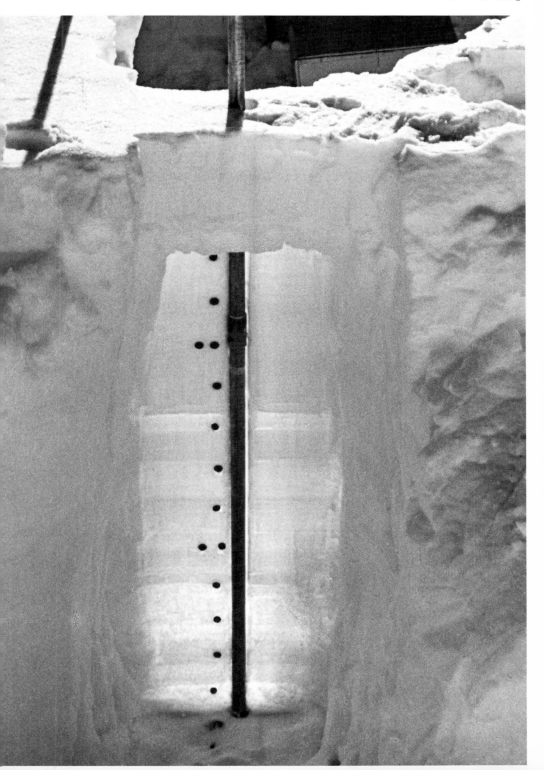

3 Snow surface formations
Surface de la neige
Superficie de la nieve
Поверхность снежного покрова
Schneeoberfläche

Snow surface formations
Surface de la neige
Superficie de la nieve
Поверхность снежного покрова
Schneeoberfläche

226

FIG. 50
Snow surface:
Smooth new-snow surface, enjoyed by skiers
(at some risk) for *wedeling.*
Location: Weissfluh, Langwies, Switzerland.

Surface de la neige:
Surface lisse de neige fraîche, appréciée par
les skieurs pour y ciseler (non sans quelques
risques) des traces en dentelle.
Lieu: Weissfluh, Langwies, Suisse.

Superficie de la nieve:
Superficie lisa de nieve nueva, disfrutada por
esquiadores (con algún riesgo) para rendi-
miento en «wedeling».
Lugar: Weissfluh, Langwies, Suiza.

Поверхность снежного покрова:
Сглаженная поверхность нового снега,
опробованная лыжниками (с некоторым
риском) для выполнения спусков.
Район: Вайсфлу/Лангвис, Швейцария

Schneeoberfläche:
Glatte Neuschneeoberfläche, von Skifahrern
(mit einigem Risiko) für Wedelabfahrten
geschätzt.
Ort: Weissfluh, Langwies, Schweiz.

Photograph: S. Gliott, EISLF.

S. Snow surface formations
S. Surface de la neige
S. Superficie de la nieve
S. Поверхность снежного покрова
S. Schneeoberfläche

Snow surface formations
Surface de la neige
Superficie de la nieve
Поверхность снежного покрова
Schneeoberfläche

228

FIG. 51
Snow surface:
Surface hoar, formed in a sequence of clear nights (negative radiation balance) by sublimation of atmospheric moisture. Unusually large crystals (see Figure 52).

Surface de la neige:
Givre de surface formé pendant une série de nuits claires (bilan de rayonnement négatif) par sublimation de l'humidité atmosphérique. Cristaux inhabituellement grands (voir fig. 52).

Superficie de la nieve:
Escarcha superficial, formada en una secuencia de noches claras (flujo de radiación negativo) mediante la sublimación de la humedad atmosférica. Cristales anormalmente grandes (véase la figura 52).

Поверхность снежного покрова:
Поверхностная изморозь. Необычайно большие кристаллы (до 15 см).

Schneeoberfläche:
Oberflächenreif, gebildet in einer Folge von klaren Nächten (negative Strahlungsbilanz) durch Sublimation von Luftfeuchtigkeit. Ungewöhnlich grosse Kristalle (siehe Fig. 52).

Photograph: E. Wengi, EISLF.

S. Snow surface formations
S. Surface de la neige
S. Superficie de la nieve
S. Поверхность снежного покрова
S. Schneeoberfläche

Snow surface formations
Surface de la neige
Superficie de la nieve
Поверхность снежного покрова
Schneeoberfläche

230

FIG. 52
Snow surface:
Surface hoar. Unusually large crystals
(up to 15 cm).

Surface de la neige:
Givre de surface. Cristaux de taille inhabi-
tuelle (allant jusqu'à 15 cm).

Superficie de la nieve:
Escarcha superficial. Cristales anormalmente
grandes (extensión hasta 15 cm).

Поверхность снежного покрова:
Поверхностная изморозь, образованная в
ясную ночь (отрицательный радиационный
баланс) путем сублимации атмосферной
влаги. Необычайно большие кристаллы
(см. след. фотографию.)

Schneeoberfläche:
Oberflächenreif. Ungewöhnlich grosse
Kristalle (bis zu 15 cm).

Photograph: E. Wengi, EISLF.

S. Snow surface formations
S. Surface de la neige
S. Superficie de la nieve
S. Поверхность снежного покрова
S. Schneeoberfläche

Snow surface formations
Surface de la neige
Superficie de la nieve
Поверхность снежного покрова
Schneeoberfläche

232

FIG. 53
Snow surface:
Soft rime deposit on snow surface. Fog, composed of supercooled droplets, was driven over the snow cover by wind from left to right.

Surface de la neige:
Dépôt de givre mou à la surface de la neige. Le brouillard, composé de gouttelettes en surfusion, était amené sur le manteau neigeux par le vent soufflant de gauche à droite.

Superficie de la nieve:
Depósito de cencellada sobre la superficie de la nieve. La niebla, compuesta de gotitas superenfriadas, fue impulsada sobre el manto nivoso por el viento que soplaba de izquierda a derecha.

Поверхность снежного покрова:
Иней, отложенный на поверхности снега. Ветер переносил туман из переохлажденных капель над снежным покровом слева направо.

Schneeoberfläche:
Rauhreifablagerung (weich) auf der Schnee-oberfläche. Aus unterkühlten Tröpfchen bestehender Nebel ist durch den Wind von links nach rechts über die Schneeoberfläche getrieben worden.

Photograph: E. Wengi, EISLF.

S. Snow surface formations
S. Surface de la neige
S. Superficie de la nieve
S. Поверхность снежного покрова
S. Schneeoberfläche

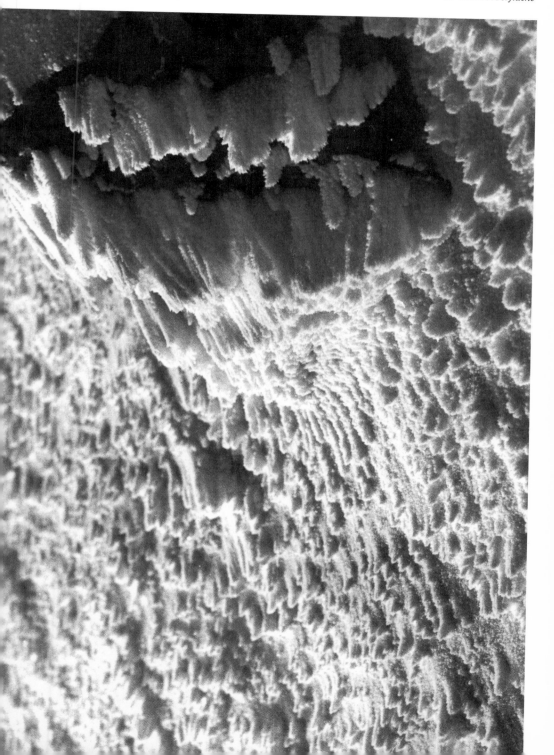

Snow surface formations
Surface de la neige
Superficie de la nieve
Поверхность снежного покрова
Schneeoberfläche

234

Fig. 54
Snow surface:
Melting and evaporating surface toothed by solar radiation. Direction of teeth: direction of main radiation flux, generally south (north) in the northern (southern) hemisphere. In low latitudes 'penitents' of considerable height may be observed.

Surface de la neige:
Surface en cours de fusion et d'évaporation dentelée par le rayonnement solaire. Direction des dents: direction du plus fort flux de rayonnement, généralement sud (nord) dans l'hémisphère nord (sud). Dans les tropiques, on peut observer des «pénitents» d'une hauteur considérable.

Superficie de la nieve:
Superficie de fusión y evaporación dentada por la radiación solar. Dirección de los dientes: dirección del flujo principal de radiación, generalmente sur (norte) en el hemisferio norte (sur). En zonas de baja latitud, pueden observarse «penitentes» de considerable altura.

Поверхность снежного покрова:
Тающая и испаряющая снежная поверхность с зазубринами, связанными с солнечной радиацией. Направление зазубрин: направление основного потока радиации, в основном северное (южное) в северном (южном) полушарии. В зонах низких широт отмечаются кающиеся значительной высоты.

Schneeoberfläche:
Schmelzende und verdampfende Schneeoberfläche, gezähnt durch Sonneneinstrahlung. Richtung der Zähne bestimmt durch die Richtung der grössten Strahlungsintensität, also allgemein gegen Süden (Norden) auf Nord-(Süd-) Hemisphäre. In Zonen niedriger Breite können sog. «Büsserschnee»-Zähne von beträchtlicher Höhe entstehen.

Photograph: E. Wengi, EISLF.

S. Snow surface formations
S. Surface de la neige
S. Superficie de la nieve
S. Поверхность снежного покрова
S. Schneeoberfläche

Snow surface formations
Surface de la neige
Superficie de la nieve
Поверхность снежного покрова
Schneeoberfläche

236

FIG. 55
Snow surface:
Film crust. Thin (1–2 mm) ice layer formed
on clean snow surface in clear weather.
Location: Weissfluhjoch/Davos, Switzerland
(EISLF experimental site).

Surface de la neige:
Mince croûte gelée. Couche de 1 à 2 mm
de glace formée sur une surface de neige
propre par temps clair.
Lieu: Weissfluhjoch/Davos, Suisse.
(Terrain d'essais de l'EISLF).

Superficie de la nieve:
Costra pelicular. Capa de hielo delgada
(1 a 2 mm) formada en una superficie de
nieve limpia en tiempo despejado.
Lugar: Weissfluhjoch/Davos, Suiza.
(Campo experimental de EISLF.)

Поверхность снежного покрова:
Ледяная пленка. Тонкий (1–2 мм) слой льда
образованный на чистой снежной поверхностью при ясной погоде.
Район: Вайсфлуйох/Давос, Швейцария
(экспериментальный участок EISLF).

Schneeoberfläche:
Firnspiegel. Dünne (1–2 mm) Eisschicht,
gebildet auf einer sauberen Schneeober-
fläche bei klarem Wetter.
Ort: Weissfluhjoch/Davos, Schweiz
(Versuchsfeld des EISLF).

Photograph: M. de Quervain, EISLF.

237

S. Snow surface formations
S. Surface de la neige
S. Superficie de la nieve
S. Поверхность снежного покрова
S. Schneeoberfläche

Snow surface formations
Surface de la neige
Superficie de la nieve
Поверхность снежного покрова
Schneeoberfläche

238

Fig. 56
Snow surface:
Film crust (foreground) ans melt teeth (back-
ground). The film crust ($\sim$1 mm thick)
is formed on clean snow in a process of
melting, evaporation and condensation under
a complex radiation flux (clear sky).
Below the protruding dry crust, melting is
in progress. The melt teeth formed in slightly
contaminated snow are oriented towards the
culmination of the sun.

Surface de la neige:
Mince croûte gelée (premier plan) et dents
de fusion (deuxième plan). La croûte mince
(environ 1 mm d'épaisseur) est formée sur de
la neige propre par un processus de fusion,
évaporation et condensation sous un flux
radiatif complexe (ciel clair). Sous la croûte
superficielle sèche, la fusion progresse.
Les dents de fusion formées dans la neige
légèrement souillée sont orientées en direction du soleil en son point culminant.

Superficie de la nieve:
Costra pelicular (primer plano) y dientes
de fusión (fondo). La costra pelicular (de un
espesor aproximado de 1 mm) se forma
sobre nieve limpia en un proceso de fusión,
evaporación y condensación bajo un flujo
de radiación complejo (cielo despejado).
Debajo de la costra seca saliente la fusión
continúa. Los dientes formados en nieve
ligeramente contaminada están orientados
hacia la culminación del sol.

Поверхность снежного покрова:
Ледяная пленка (на переднем плане) и
зазубрины таяния (на заднем плане).
Ледяная пленка (толщина 1 мм) образо-
валась в процессе таяния, испарения и
конденсации на чистой снежной поверхности в условиях сложного радиационного
баланса (чистое небо). Ниже выступает
развивающаяся сухая кора таяния.
Зазубрины таяния образовались в слегка
загрязненном снегу и ориентированы по
отношению к наивысшему положению
солнца.

Schneeoberfläche:
Firnspiegel (Vordergrund) und Schmelz-
zähne (Hintergrund). Der Firnspiegel
(ca. 1 mm dick) bildet sich auf einer sauberen
Schneeoberfläche durch Schmelzen,
Verdampfen und Kondensation unter einer
komplexen Strahlungsbilanz (bei klarem
Himmel). Unter dem hervortretenden trok-
kenen Eisfilm schmilzt der Schnee. Die
Schmelzzähne, die bei leicht verunreinigtem
Schnee entstehen, sind gegen den Sonnen-
höchststand gerichtet.

Photograph: M. de Quervain, EISLF.

S. Snow surface formations
S. Surface de la neige
S. Superficie de la nieve
S. Поверхность снежного покрова
S. Schneeoberfläche

Snow surface formations
Surface de la neige
Superficie de la nieve
Поверхность снежного покрова
Schneeoberfläche

240

Fig. 57
Snow surface:
Hard ice crust formed on snow surface after rainfall with subsequent or simultaneous rapid freezing.

Surface de la neige:
Croûte dure de glace formée sur la surface de la neige sous une pluie gelée immédiatement ou peu après sa chute.

Superficie de la nieve:
Costra de hielo duro formado sobre la superficie de nieve después de la lluvia, por congelación rápida o inmediata.

Поверхность снежного покрова:
Твердая ледяная корка на снежной поверхности после дождя с последующим или одновременным замерзанием воды.

Schneeoberfläche:
Harte Eiskruste, gebildet auf der Schneeoberfläche durch einen gleichzeitig oder unmittelbar anschliessend gefrierenden Regen.

Photograph: L. Rey, France.

S. *Snow surface formations*
S. *Surface de la neige*
S. *Superficie de la nieve*
S. *Поверхность снежного покрова*
S. *Schneeoberfläche*

Snow surface formations
Surface de la neige
Superficie de la nieve
Поверхность снежного покрова
Schneeoberfläche

242

FIG. 58
Snow surface:
Wind ripples formed by 'blowing snow'.
Depth of layer of airborne particles only
about 10 cm.
Location: Weissfluhjoch/Davos,
Switzerland.

Surface de la neige:
Rides au vent formées par la «neige souf-
flée»; l'épaisseur de la couche de neige ventée
n'est que de 10 cm.
Lieu: Weissfluhjoch/Davos, Suisse.

Superficie de la nieve:
Ondulaciones en la superficie de la nieve
formadas por ventisca; la profundidad de la
capa de partículas suspendidas en el aire es
solamente de unos 10 cm.
Lugar: Weissfluhjoch/Davos, Suiza.

Поверхность снежного покрова:
Ветровая рябь образованная метелевым
снегом, высота слоя поднятых ветром
частиц только около 10 см.
Район: Вайсфлуйох/Давос, Швейцария

Schneeoberfläche:
Windrippen gebildet durch Schneefegen.
Schicht der suspendierten Schneeteilchen
nur etwa 10 cm tief.
Ort: Weissfluhjoch/Davos, Schweiz.

Photograph: E. Wengi, EISLF.

S. Snow surface formations
S. Surface de la neige
S. Superficie de la nieve
S. Поверхность снежного покрова
S. Schneeoberfläche

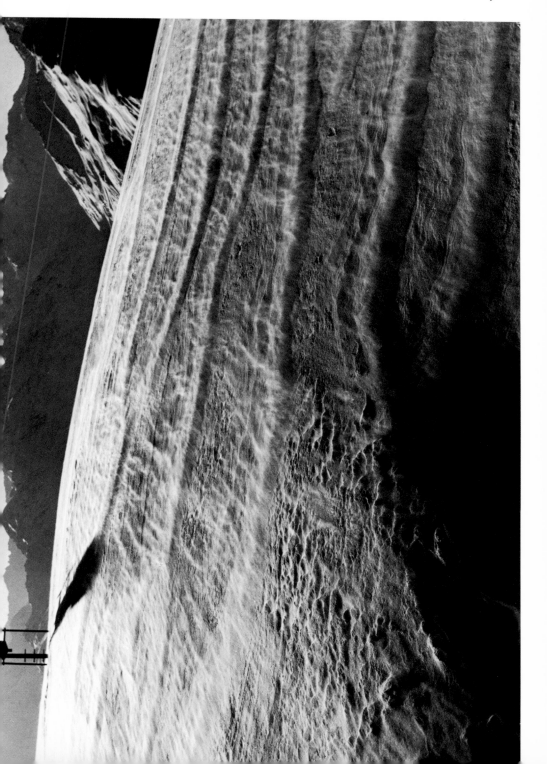

Snow surface formations
Surface de la neige
Superficie de la nieve
Поверхность снежного покрова
Schneeoberfläche

244

Fig. 59
Snow surface:
Drift deposit in the neighbourhood of a
building located behind the photographer.
Location: Weissfluhjoch/Davos,
Switzerland.

Поверхность снежного покрова:
Снежные отложения вблизи строений,
расположенных за спиной фотографа.
Район: Вайсфлуйох/Давос, Швейцария

Surface de la neige:
Congère formée au voisinage d'un bâtiment
situé dans le dos du photographe.
Lieu: Weissfluhjoch/Davos, Suisse.

Schneeoberfläche:
Treibschneeablagerung in der Nähe eines
Gebäudes (im Rücken des Photographen).
Ort: Weissfluhjoch/Davos, Schweiz.

Superficie de la nieve:
Depósito formado por ventisca en la
proximidad de un edificio situado a la
espalda del fotógrafo.
Lugar: Weissfluhjoch/Davos, Suiza.

Photograph: E. Wengi, EISLF.

S. *Snow surface formations*
S. *Surface de la neige*
S. *Superficie de la nieve*
S. *Поверхность снежного покрова*
S. *Schneeoberfläche*

Snow surface formations
Surface de la neige
Superficie de la nieve
Поверхность снежного покрова
Schneeoberfläche

F<small>IG.</small> 60
Snow surface:
Irregular wind erosion and deposit, called
sastrugi.

Surface de la neige:
Erosion éolienne et dépôts irréguliers appelés
«sastrugi».

Superficie de la nieve:
Depósito y erosión irregular debidos
al viento, denominado «sastrugi».

Поверхность снежного покрова:
Неровности образованные ветровой
эрозией и метелевыми отложениями, так
называемые заструги.

Schneeoberfläche:
Unregelmässige Wind-Erosion und
-Ablagerung, sog. «Sastrugi».

Photograph: E. Wengi, EISLF.

S. Snow surface formations
S. Surface de la neige
S. Superficie de la nieve
S. Поверхность снежного покрова
S. Schneeoberfläche

Snow surface formations
Surface de la neige
Superficie de la nieve
Поверхность снежного покрова
Schneeoberfläche

Fɪɢ. 61
Snow surface:
Melt channels (on slope) and melt funnels
(on flat terrain) produced by rain or melt
water.

Surface de la neige:
Rigoles de fusion (sur la pente) et entonnoirs
de fusion (en terrain plat) produits par la
pluie ou par l'eau de fonte.

Superficie de la nieve:
Canales de fusión (en la pendiente) y
embudos de fusión (en el terreno plano)
producidos por la lluvia o por el agua de
deshielo.

Поверхность снежного покрова:
Борозды таяния (на склоне) и воронки
таяния (на плоской поверхности), образованные во время дождя или тающей водой.

Schneeoberfläche:
Schmelzrinnen (am Hang) und Schmelz-
trichter (auf der Ebene) erzeugt durch Regen
oder Schmelzwasser.

Photograph: E. Wengi, EISLF.

S. Snow surface formations
S. Surface de la neige
S. Superficie de la nieve
S. Поверхность снежного покрова
S. Schneeoberfläche

4 Special formations

Formations spéciales

Formaciones especiales

Особые образования

Spezielle Bildungen

Special formations
Formations spéciales
Formaciones especiales
Особые образования (прочие движения снега, связанные с лавинами)
Spezielle Bildungen

FIG. 62
Slow movement of snow cover:
Creeping movement within the snow cover
superimposed upon settling movement,
demonstrated in a snow profile. A vertical
hole filled with sawdust, originally located
in the position marked with the sounding
probe (left), was found after forty days in
a slanting position.

Mouvements lents du manteau neigeux:
Glissement du manteau neigeux superposé
au tassement. Mise en évidence par un profil
de neige: un tracé vertical, rempli de sciure,
était à l'origine dans la position matérialisée
par la sonde (à gauche); on l'a trouvé après
40 jours dans la position oblique.

Movimiento lento del manto nivoso:
Movimiento de reptación dentro del
manto nivoso superpuesto por el
movimiento de asentamiento, demostrado en
un perfil de nieve. Un orificio vertical lleno
con serrín, situado originalmente en la
posición marcada con la sonda de prueba
(izquierda), fue encontrado después de
40 días en posición oblicua.

Медленное движение снежного покрова:
Движение сползания, наложенное на движение оседания внутри снежного покрова,
показано на разрезе. Вертикальная
скважина была заполнена красящим
веществом и первоначально располагалась
вертикально (см. слева), изогнутая кривая
получена через 40 дней.

Langsame Schneebewegung:
Kriechbewegung innerhalb der Schneedecke
überlagert der Setzungsbewegung, demon-
striert in einem Schneeprofil. Ein vertikales
mit Sägemehl gefülltes Loch, das sich anfäng-
lich an der mit einer Sondierstange bezeich-
neten Stelle links befand, wird nach 40 Tagen
in einer schiefen Lage angetroffen.

Photograph: H. Frutiger, EISLF.

P. *Slow movement of snow cover*
P. *Mouvements lents du manteau neigeux*
P. *Movimiento lento del manto nivoso*
P. *Медленное движение снежного покрова*
P. *Langsame Schneebewegung*

Special formations
Formations spéciales
Formaciones especiales
Особые образования (прочие движения снега, связанные с лавинами)
Spezielle Bildungen

Fig. 63
Slow movement of snow cover:
Slow gliding movement of a wet snow cover on smooth ground produces cracks (glide mouths).

Mouvements lents du manteau neigeux:
Le lent glissement du manteau neigeux humide sur un sol lisse produit des fissures (fentes de glissement).

Movimiento lento del manto nivoso:
El movimiento deslizante lento del manto nivoso húmedo sobre el terreno liso produce grietas (bocas de deslizamiento).

Медленное движение снежного покрова:
Медленное скольжение влажного снежного покрова по сглаженной поверхности грунта с образованием трещин («пасти скольжения»).

Langsame Schneebewegung:
Eine langsame Gleitbewegung der nassen Schneedecke auf einer glatten Unterlage erzeugt Spalten (Gleitmäuler).

Photograph: M. Shoda, Japan.

P. *Slow movement of snow cover*
P. *Mouvements lents du manteau neigeux*
P. *Movimiento lento del manto nivoso*
P. *Медленное движение снежного покрова*
P. *Langsame Schneebewegung*

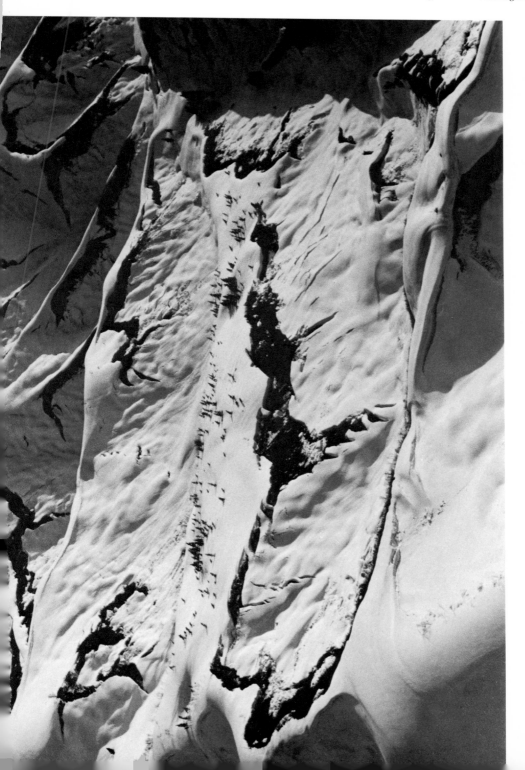

Fig. 64

Slow movement of snow cover:
Glide crevasse in snow cover, gradually widening. Snowfall has marked a first phase of the opening. The lower, dark zone represents the movement after snowfall had ceased.

Mouvements lents du manteau neigeux:
Fissure provoquée par le glissement et s'ouvrant lentement. Une chute de neige a marqué une première phase de la fissuration. La partie inférieure sombre représente le progrès du mouvement après la fin de la chute de neige.

Movimiento lento del manto nivoso:
La grieta de deslizamiento en el manto nivoso se va ensanchando gradualmente. La caída de nieve ha marcado una primera fase de la apertura. La zona inferior más oscura representa el movimiento después que ha dejado de nevar.

Медленное движение снежного покрова:
Постепенно расширяющаяся трещина скольжения в снежном покрове. Снегопад маркировал первую фазу раскрытия. Нижняя темная зона отмечает движение после прекращения снегопада.

Langsame Schneebewegung:
Gleitspalte in der Schneedecke sich langsam ausweitend. Die untere, dunkle Zone zeigt die nach Beendigung eines Schneefalls eingetretene Verschiebung.

Photograph: M. Shoda, Japan.

P. Slow movement of snow cover
P. Mouvements lents du manteau neigeux
P. Movimiento lento del manto nivoso
P. Медленное движение снежного покрова
P. Langsame Schneebewegung

Special formations
Formations spéciales
Formaciones especiales
Особые образования (прочие движения снега, связанные с лавинами)
Spezielle Bildungen

FIG. 65
Slow movement of snow cover:
Fold produced in slowly gliding wet snow
on smooth terrain (grass). On the downhill
side the movement is prevented by enhanced
roughness of terrain.

Mouvements lents du manteau neigeux:
Plissement provoqué par le glissement lent
de la neige humide sur un sol lisse (herbe).
Vers le bas de la pente ce mouvement est
contrarié par une plus grande rugosité du sol.

Movimiento lento del manto nivoso:
Pliegue producido en nieve húmeda que se
desliza lentamente sobre terreno liso (hierba).
Pendiente abajo, el movimiento se ve
impedido por la mayor rugosidad del
terreno.

Медленное движение снежного покрова:
Складка, образованная медленным скольжением влажного снега по сглаженной
поверхности (траве). Ниже по склону
движению препятствует повышенная
шероховатость поверхности.

Langsame Schneebewegung:
Falte erzeugt durch langsam auf glattem
Gelände (Gras) gleitenden Schnee. Talseits
ist die Bewegung durch erhöhte Bodenrauhigkeit verhindert.

Photograph: M. de Quervain, EISLF.

P. Slow movement of snow cover
P. Mouvements lents du manteau neigeux
P. Movimiento lento del manto nivoso
P. Медленное движение снежного покрова
P. Langsame Schneebewegung

Special formations
Formations spéciales
Formaciones especiales
Особые образования (прочие движения снега, связанные с лавинами)
Spezielle Bildungen

FIG. 66
Slow movement of snow cover:
Slowly gliding snow layer picks up a thin
blanket of new snow covering a previously
formed glide mouth and rolls it up like a
carpet (rare phenomenon).

Mouvements lents du manteau neigeux:
Une couche de neige glissant lentement
entraîne une mince couverture de neige
fraîche couvrant une fente de glissement
formée précédemment et la roule à la manière
d'un tapis (phénomène rare).

Movimiento lento del manto nivoso:
La capa de nieve de deslizamiento lento
recoge la delgada capa de nieve nueva que
cubre una boca de deslizamiento previamente
formada y la enrolla como una alfombra
(fenómeno raro).

Карнизы:
Перенос снега ветром при отсутствии
снегопада приводит к неравномерному
распределению снега и образованию
карнизов. Снежные флаги на гребне выше
роста человека.
Район: Вайсфлуйох/Давос, Швейцария.

Langsame Schneebewegung:
Eine langsam gleitende Schneelage erfasst
eine dünne Neuschneeschicht, die ein früher
gebildetes Gleitmaul bedeckt, und rollt sie
auf wie einen Teppich (seltene Erscheinung!).

Photograph: H. in der Gand, EISLF.

P. *Slow movement of snow cover*
P. *Mouvements lents du manteau neigeux*
P. *Movimiento lento del manto nivoso*
P. *Медленное движение снежного покрова*
P. *Langsame Schneebewegung*

Special formations
Formations spéciales
Formaciones especiales
Особые образования (прочие движжения снега, связанные с лавинами)
Spezielle Bildungen

FIG. 67
Cornices:
Snowdrift in the absence of snowfall resulting
in unequal snow deposit and cornices. Snow
flag taller than a man on downwind side of
a ridge.
Location: Weissfluhjoch/Davos,
Switzerland.

Corniches:
La reprise de la neige par le vent en l'absence
de précipitation provoque un dépôt inégal de
la neige ainsi que des corniches. Le surplomb
de neige côté sous le vent d'une crête peut
être plus haut que la taille d'un homme.
Lieu: Weissfluhjoch/Davos, Suisse.

Cornisas:
El arrastre de la nieve en ausencia de nevada,
da como resultado cornisas y una deposición desigual de la nieve. Bandera de nieve
más alta que un hombre, en el lado de
sotavento de una cresta.
Lugar: Weissfluhjoch/Davos, Suiza.

Медленное движжение снежного покрова:
Медленно скользящий слой снега захваты-
вает тонкий покров нового снега, покры-
вающего первоначально образованные
участки трещин, и скатывает их подобно
скатыванию ковра (очень редкое явление).

Wächten:
Schneetreiben ohne Neuschneefall, eine
ungleichmässige Schneeablagerung und
Wächten erzeugend. Die Schneefahne
leeseitig des Kammes ist mehr als manns-
hoch.
Ort: Weissfluhjoch/Davos, Schweiz.

Photograph: E. Wengi, EISLF.

Special formations
Formations spéciales
Formaciones especiales
Особые образования (прочие движения снега, связанные с лавинами)
Spezielle Bildungen

Fig. 68
Cornices:
Cornice protruding on the downwind (lee) side of a ridge. The formation is particularly pronounced if the upwind slope is less inclined than the downwind slope.

Corniches:
Corniches avançant au-dessus du côté sous le vent d'une crête. Cette formation est particulièrement prononcée si le côté au vent est moins incliné que le côté sous le vent.

Cornisas:
Cornisa que sobresale en el lado de sotavento de una cordillera. La formación es particularmente pronunciada si la pendiente de barlovento es menos inclinada que la pendiente de sotavento.

Карнизы:
Карнизы на подветренной стороне гребня. Эти образования особенно хорошо выражены, если наветренный склон менее крут, чем подветренный.

Wächten:
Wächte leeseitig eines Grates vorkragend. Die Bildung ist besonders ausgeprägt, wenn der windseitige Hang weniger geneigt ist als der windabgekehrte.

Photograph: M. Shoda, Japan.

Addresses of photographers
Adresses des photographes
Direcciones de los fotógrafos
Адреса фотографов
Adressen der Photographen

Alpine Luftbild	Innsbruck, Austria
ATP Bilderdienst	Ringier, Zürich, Switzerland
Dorsaz, R.[3]	Sierre, Switzerland
EISLF:[3]	E. Bucher, H. Etter, H. Frutiger[1], R. Figilister, S. Gliott, H. in der Gand, J. Neher, M. de Quervain, A. Roch, M. Schild, E. Sommerhalder, E. Wengi. Federal Institute for Snow and Avalanches Research, Weissfluhjoch/Davos, Switzerland
Engelberger,[2]	Stans, Switzerland
LaChapelle, E. R.[3]	Department of Atmospheric Sciences, University of Washington, Seattle, Wash., United States
Ludwig, R.	Mayrhofen, Austria
Meerkämper, M.	Davos-Platz, Switzerland
Onodera, H.[3]	Faculty of Agriculture, Hokkaido University, Sapporo, Hokkaido, Japan
Perren, B.[2]	Zermatt, Switzerland
Porton, W.	Scuol, Switzerland
Rey, L.[3]	CEN, Météorologie Nationale, Grenoble, France
Saxer, E.	Adligenswil, Switzerland (deceased)
Shoda, M.[3]	Nagaoka, Japan (deceased 1974)

1. At the time of the photographs, H. Frutiger was with the Institute for Disaster Prevention, United States Forest Range and Experiment Station, Fort Collins, Colo., United States.
2. Photographs provided by EISLF.
3. The photographers so indicated generously gave free permission for the reproduction of their pictures in this atlas.